Living at <u>316</u>

Sylvia Steele-Dunn

WestBow
PRESS
A DIVISION OF THOMAS NELSON

WestBow Press books may be ordered through booksellers or by contacting:

WestBow Press
A Division of Thomas Nelson
1663 Liberty Drive
Bloomington, IN 47403
www.westbowpress.com
1 (866) 928-1240

Because of the dynamic nature of the Internet, any web addresses or links contained in this book may have changed since publication and may no longer be valid. The views expressed in this work are solely those of the author and do not necessarily reflect the views of the publisher, and the publisher hereby disclaims any responsibility for them.

Any people depicted in stock imagery provided by Thinkstock are models, and such images are being used for illustrative purposes only.

Certain stock imagery © Thinkstock.

ISBN: 978-1-4497-7997-9 (sc)
ISBN: 978-1-4497-7998-6 (hc)
ISBN: 978-1-4497-7999-3 (e)

Library of Congress Control Number: 2012923916

Unless otherwise indicated, all Scripture quotations are taken from the New American Standard version of the Bible.

FOR INFORMATION CONTACT:
Sylvia Steele-Dunn, Huntsville, AL 35824
Printed in the United States of America

WestBow Press rev. date: 12/27/2012

Genesis 1:1

In the beginning God …

John 3:16

So loved the world that He gave …

Revelation 22:21

The grace of the Lord Jesus …

The

book ends

and

foundation

that hold me together

Dedicated to the loving memory of my precious baby sister, Cindy Arlene Steele-Miner.

This is not a tell-all.
All cannot be told.
All should not be told.

This is a testimony
about arriving at a conscious decision
to deliver a mandate.

It is about getting to the root of it all
and embracing the spiritual journey
while examining the soil.

It is about being at peace with it all,
stepping out on faith, and
cultivating the good seed
initially planted in a firm foundation
of
love.

I am
my Father's daughter …

I choose
to be healed.

ACKNOWLEDGMENTS

Above all I thank and praise my God.

This writing is poured out of much love and respect for the lives and memories of my grandma and grandpa Gibson. They scooped us up and took us to Sunday school, church, plays, and to hear the message of Reverend Billy Graham.

For the blessing of my husband, Frank Dunn, and children, Jerrin and Jeanine, I am always thankful. My family has seen and loved me through the best and worst of times. The journey to understanding and giving unconditional love has been realized through each of them. Love you dearly!

Much love and respect to Momma and Daddy. Because they endured, we are. Their love and nurturing is composed of all that was required to hold, heal, sustain, and love us unconditionally. I love my precious sisters, brothers, to life. My Dunn family of Charleston, Tennessee, and loving memory of my precious father-in-law Bo, thank you for teaching me another dimension of love and acceptance.

Very special thank-you to Mary Lacey, and "Cuz" Cynthia Harris for their labor of love in supporting me and pouring over initial manuscripts. I am forever thankful for your gifts. Iron indeed sharpens iron!

Contents

Preface

My bedside alarm clock is always set ten minutes ahead. This allows for snooze time. It is barely Saturday morning, and it has happened again, for probably the third time this week. I've awakened in the middle of the night to the luminous digital display. It is 3:16 a.m. Again, 3:16. I stare, wondering, *Why am I always waking at 3:16 a.m.? Why do I find myself turning in the afternoons to check the time, only to discover it is 3:16?*

This is my conclusion—and there is no sense in fighting against or questioning it any further—it's in my DNA to live at 3:16! It's also in my nature to understand why I must live there. I must articulate why I choose to live there.

CHAPTER 1

Nehemiah 3:16

After him Nehemiah the son of Azbuk, official of half the district of Bethzur, made repairs as far as a point opposite the tombs of David, and as far as the artificial pool and the house of the mighty men.

Standing in Need of Repair

Freedom comes when you go back to the root and identify the seed. There is a name attached to the seed. So I finally begin reflecting, writing, and advancing.

This writing was conceived eight years ago, eighty-six hundred miles from home. I was onboard the aircraft carrier USS *George Washington*, on a self-imposed lockdown, snuggled in my top rack, studying for Sunday worship service. Sunday was Mother's Day, and I was gathering final thoughts on a sermon I titled "Don't Blame Momma … Them's Daddy's Kids!" It was a message about the stubborn children of Israel and how Moses got so fed up with their murmuring and complaining that he went to God and said (in my words) "Look Lord! These children you gave me? They are really working my nerves here!"

As I studied and jotted down speaking points, childhood memories came rushing in and overtook me. Thumbing through my Bible I discovered a pattern in the Scripture that I knew was speaking to me and moving me to a place I had not entered before. I wrote three pages of Scripture and summary thoughts that surfaced for each scriptural reference. Then, deep into the night, in the belly of the ship, I secured the paper in my Bible. Weeks later, before returning home from sea, I discovered that these notes read like an outline. I decided it was a book outline. That book would be titled *Living at 316*.

Sometime after returning to the States in late 2004, I shared the outline with my sister Sherrie. From time to time Sherrie would ask, "Sissy, what happened to *Living at 316?*"

All I could say was, "It is going to happen." The when and how were unknown, but I knew it would come to pass.

For seven long years I would look over the notes from time to time, jotting down thoughts and pondering, questioning myself as to why I was not moving forward with the book. It wasn't until the eighth year that the real purpose of this excavation became crystal clear.

July 2011, in the seventh year of this book's pregnancy, I was praying, *Lord. I need help. Please show me what I am to do with this book idea. I cannot shake it. I need a sign. Am I still supposed to write Living at 316?* The very next day, I received a text message from my cousin Cynthia in Corona, California. She e-mailed a small group of family members.

The night prior to sending this message, Cynthia had a sharp dream about our Gibson family. At one point in the dream my baby sister, Cindy (who had just passed a month earlier), spoke to Cousin Cynthia. Cindy was standing in front of the house we grew up in, 316 Wood Street, Wheaton, Illinois. Cindy pointed to the house and said, "Tell this."

Without a doubt I knew my prayer was answered. That part of Cynthia's dream was for me. I will always believe that to be true if for no other reason than the timing of her dream. It immediately moved me to action. I began to pull all my notes together again. Notes were tucked into Bibles, journals, and dresser drawers. There was so much to gather. I had been carrying this baby a long time, and it felt like the third trimester of a pregnancy. This baby had dropped into birthing position. Continuing to travail, I felt overwhelmed with expectation that the time had come to birth spirit into the natural. Long pregnancies can be extremely uncomfortable. All labor pains are not the same.

The prophet Jeremiah was known as "the weeping prophet" because of the people's need for repentance and turning back to God.

The prophet Nehemiah is known for successfully leading the rebuilding of the temple. He had been deeply distressed over the neglect and destruction of the temple of God. For the ancient Israelites, The "Holy Place" was where the Spirit of the Lord dwelled and the people worshipped the almighty God.

I still needed repentance and repair.

Who Can You Trust when You Are Broken?

Trust the only One who can turn you inside out to restore you right side up.

CHAPTER 2

Genesis 3:16

To the woman He said, "I will greatly multiply your pain in childbirth. In pain you will bring forth children; Yet your desire will be for your husband, and he will rule over you."

Birthing Pains

A reread of Genesis 3:16 brought on a flood of the same torment that controlled me as a child. Loving all things church and wanting to understand the Bible from a very young age, I was often confused. Then there was the inner struggle, being driven by a secret so dark no one could be told. It was the common struggle of good versus evil.

In trying hard to unfold the meaning of the Bible, I stayed lost in Genesis in what seemed like forever. Here's what I got at the age of ten: (1) birth cannot come without distress; (2) the woman messed up everything by her direct defiance of both God's and husband's authority; and (3) this was God's decision, and that was final. Why? Because God is God, and the preachers consistently said God alone is sovereign.

Even as a child, I wrestled with the garden story. It continued to replay in my head. I imagined how I would have handled Adam and Eve back then. And, of course, we can all be eternally grateful that I am not God! Yet in my childish head, I recall rehearsing how I would have said something like this: "I will greatly increase the animals you have to feed, smell, and clean up after, have a good day, enjoy the garden. Oh, and by the way, I double dog dare you to touch that tree again!" Yes! That would have fixed their little wagons.

I want you to appreciate that as a ten-year-old girl, I would sit for hours trying to understand the King James Bible. I was seeking.

As I studied the third chapter of Genesis as a child, I recall the feeling that this just didn't seem fair at all; the woman got demoted and the man got a job promotion. Wow! Great. Downhill they went. Later, as a teenager still trying to figure out Genesis, I'd think, *This guy couldn't even control one woman, and he gets an eternal appointment! The entire nation of Israel messed up on a regular basis, and they remained chosen!*

These are the wild things that used to run through my adolescent head when I attempted to study my Bible. There is no telling how many times I read the book of Genesis. I would always get to this point and think long and hard about whether life was some sort of setup or if this story was actually inspired by God. I sort of believed some male chauvinist with a whole lot of authority who justified putting his little spin on things wrote this part. After all, who was documenting these conversations word for word? You didn't question the Holy Bible, or any authority figure in the church for that matter. I learned that all questions weren't tolerated. I learned that my struggle with sin was a private issue, even if my reputation played out publicly. My ten-year-old self was struggling with great sin. I would ask certain questions in hope that my mother or father would engage in dialogue that would allow me to safely open up, but that didn't happen. Eventually, I just got baptized and tried to wash away guilt and pain.

More of what I read in Genesis concerned me. For example, Scriptures like Genesis 3:6 that reads, "and when the woman saw that the tree was good for food, and that it was pleasant to the eyes, and a tree to be desired to make one wise, she took of the fruit thereof, and did eat, and gave also unto her husband with her; and he did eat." What! Okay, see, that's the part that used to make me think *hmmmm*.

The New Living Translation reads, "who was with her." *So Adam was with her,* I would think, while she stood there conversing with a slick serpent, quoting what thus saith the Lord! Adam doesn't speak up and say something like, "What did my wife just tell you buddy? Get lost." That's what my father would have said ... just before he shot him.

Scripture does not say Eve left the serpent's presence, located Adam, and then shared the fruit of the Tree of Knowledge with him. It always seemed to me that Adam was right there relatively close to Eve while she conversed with this straight, standing enemy (the serpent doesn't go on his belly until verse 14). Why doesn't Adam stop his wife from conversing with this dude? And why have I never heard it preached that way? I never could figure out why no one ever raised this point in Bible study!

I eventually learned that there were some life experiences that were safest and best kept to myself. Somewhere along the way, I concluded that some spiritual questions should be treated the same. Just tuck them away and wait for God, because no one down here really cares.

I overthought everything. That probably explains childhood

migraines and nosebleeds. Baby boomers are thinkers, but my questioning was not unique. Most children raise questions like, "Where did I come from?" and "Why" certain things happen. It's how they learn.

My baby sister once told me that our mother said this about me: "Sissy was the type of child that wanted to know stuff. She needed to have conversation. I neither had the time nor took the time that she required. If I had to do it again, I would spend more time with all my children and pay closer attention to what was really going on with each one of them." True, I was curious, and no one seemed to be paying close attention. I was always searching for dialogue and escape routes.

Regardless of the questions that swirled in my head, I believe I grasped the overriding theme of Genesis early on. *In the beginning of time in this universe and on this earth, God created all that is. God is in control. Stories are necessary to explain how things came to be.*

Genesis contains all the characteristics of a good novel: explaining origin of a star bloodline, survival of the same, struggle, murder, a hero, wayward and disobedient children, and a loving, forgiving, sometimes fed-up father. As I continued reading the Old Testament it was apparent the Father prefers to love his children, those kids created in *His image.*

The childhood demanded a review. It wasn't until I was nearly forty years old and pursing a bachelor degree in religion that I finally went back and revisited my childhood understanding of Genesis. And now, as an adult who has been through some things, I saw the teaching and wisdom of the Old Testament Scriptures in a whole new light. Actually, some things I was going through at the time had seriously rocked my adult world and forced me to look at the totality of my life, including my actions, thought processes, and heart condition.

Layers were identified; layers of "stuff" on top of "me," the child walking around in an adult body. And for the first time, I gave myself permission to be okay with the things I questioned as a child, okay with who I had become, and okay with starting the process of killing off the dark shadows that lurked for decades. The healing process was long overdue. Much of me was not yet settled. Although I had many positive experiences—a successful military career, beautiful family—I was still doing what I had done since childhood: operating on autopilot, loving unconditionally, and being intimidated by anything that asserted power over me. With all of that, I still was not sure what I wanted to be when I grew up.

During undergraduate study, one class became a true catalyst. It was "The Life and Writings of Paul" and Dr. Singletary was my professor. It just didn't seem that Dr. Singletary cared much for me, but it really didn't matter, because I had fallen in love with the apostle Paul, and I was getting what I needed from the class. The New Testament made so much more sense to me than the Old Testament. I could identify with the passion and zeal Paul had for declaring the Word of God. It was based on personal experience. He had studied, but all of that meant nothing in comparison to his personal experience and conversion.

An assignment came to write a personal creed. The objective was to identify the journey that led to your overall core beliefs and power center. There was rebirth I never saw coming. There was newness and desire to add up all things God had blessed me with and all the persons He had placed in my life. The good, bad, and very ugly were identified. A fresh season of pruning had begun, and the cutting was painful.

When the time came to present my personal creed to the class, I was both strong and heavy of heart. I was speaking to strangers about cares that lay dormant and heavy in a shallow trench since adolescence. In speaking to the class, I teared up several times but was able to press through to completion. It was like I was being pushed out of a place I didn't want to abandon, like being forced through a tight birth canal. I thanked God for the time limit Dr. Singletary placed on the presentation assignment.

I had landed at an appointed time.

As I walked back to my seat, Dr. Singletary gently grabbed my left arm, looked over the top of his glasses, stared straight into my face and said, "Young lady, you tell your story as loud and as often as you possible can."

You could have knocked me over with a feather. There had been a conversation. It was a brief conversation—one exchange. I understood exactly what had happened. Once again the ruling Husband gripped the bride, and this bride was still very childish.

Little Boys and Girls Need Both Mommy and Daddy

Love begins at home. If only more value were placed on positive experiences and communication with our children, our children would not fail as often.

CHAPTER 3

Exodus 3:16

"Go and gather the elders of Israel together and say
to them, "The LORD, the God of your fathers,
the God of Abraham, Isaac and Jacob, has appeared
to me, saying, 'I am indeed concerned about you
and what has been done to you in Egypt.'"

House of Distress

Now I embrace the years of growing up at 316 Wood Street
and celebrate God's unfolding plan for my life. It would be easy
to feel victimized by many of the experiences, but that would
be wasted energy. Pointing a finger of blame is no longer an
exercise. Besides, the finger also points to me. I reflect mostly
in search of truth and to see if I learned from the lessons that
were presented in my journey. I am especially thankful for
those events that broadened my mind and stretched me beyond
the comfort zone of Wheaton.

We've heard of persons molested by parents, siblings, and
relatives, but never have I heard anyone tell of being molested
by three persons over a period of years. I may never know of
others who endured what I went through, but I believe they

are out there. The reality is such a thing is both shameful and embarrassing. My home was not the place of the incest—for me it was not father or siblings—but 316 Wood Street was where I silently suffered, enduring the stench of the actions done against me and the embarrassment of later being a willing participant. My home was not safe enough to ask for help.

On bad days, I would sit on the sofa for hours, feeling trapped and wondering how God could be such a good and loving Father and allow so much pain and suffering in the world. From the morning news of Vietnam casualty updates to bracing for casualties in our home, I learned chaos and suffering were everywhere. And who had time to labor in correcting the world's condition when home was a battlefield? How could our mother represent stability and calm in church every Sunday and then return home to fight against a fortified enemy, whose weekly assault recharged on Sundays and distressed the atmosphere throughout the week. Where exactly was God in all of this?

I lived on the edge of sanity, always waiting for the signal or alarm that the bottom had finally and indeed fallen out. At night I would lay in bed, listening to the Chicago North Western trains going back and forth on the tracks and wishing I could ride that train far away from Wheaton.

I experienced years of recurring nightmares as a child. Upon closing my eyes at night, I instantly knew if I was going to have the nightmare or one of two other persistent dreams. The nightmares always started the same. If my eyes closed and I saw swirling dark colors—black, purple, and blue—I immediately froze as if paralyzed, while fear sucked me in. Then giant birds with large, sharp, and shiny needles would chase my sister Sherrie and I. We would run as fast as we could and eventually dive into a ditch, where we were safe. I often woke up and ran into Mom and Dad's room. Who knew how long they permitted me to stay there, but it was probably until I fell back asleep. This was magical to me—the fact that I was somehow back in my own bed in the morning; I can recall being amazed by it. At some point though, it became clear that Daddy returned me to my bed during the night.

If I closed my eyes and the darkness didn't come, my favorite dream might start right away. In the first good dream, I would be sitting up in bed while a little girl led a beautiful parade down from the top of the robe closet and onto the bed. This was a happy dream, full of pretty colors.

The third dream was about the rapture. I would envision the end of the world. Jesus was coming down from the sky. And that was the most I remember of that dream. This dream apparently came from all of the fiery heaven or hell preaching we sat under in those days.

It always seemed bizarre to have these repetitive dreams, and they lasted for years. As a matter of fact, the scary dark dream did not end until I was eighteen years old and moved out of my parents' house. I thought it had to be directly related to my vivid imagination and personal craziness. I never asked my brothers and sisters if they had similar dreams. I just assumed they did not.

Another thing that happened at night was a lot of fighting and arguing between my parents. Whenever the loud voices woke me, I'd react the same. I would sneak out of bed and around the corner and sit behind a wall, next to the dirty clothes hamper, and listen. I hung onto every word I understood. And I would cry and internalize it all. This is something I did as early as six or seven years old. The consequence was I heard a lot of mess that was personal, hateful, scary, and damaging. It taught me to internalize negativity and absorb instead of deflect life's fiery darts.

If there was total quiet in the house, it was probably because you were lucky enough to be home alone.

I believe a lot of the chaos stemmed from my parents' realization that they, too, were trapped—with children, each other, and themselves. I can see how young families fall apart. You try to create a stable family out of what you salvaged from your own brokenness. It is a recipe for fear and failure.

Our home atmosphere was often extreme, swinging from love, laughter, and singing to drunkenness, screaming, and fighting in what seemed like a heartbeat. If Dad was high, we had to "tip lightly," which meant hold the noise down while Dad kicked back in his recliner. In the winter, I preferred to sit behind my dad's chair, right on top of the floor heat vent. Other times I would sit close to Daddy's feet. All of us kids liked to be the first one to respond in case Dad asked someone to pull off his shoes. That's what he usually did after he stumbled in the house drunk each evening. If he didn't go straight to his bedroom, he would plop in his easy chair and have somebody pull his shoes off. While Daddy was in the house, you better be quiet—sit still and keep quiet. If not, all heck would break loose. This was really difficult, seeing as there were six of us: three boys, three girls. We were silly kids, loved to have fun, and loved to laugh, so you know we got yelled at often.

How in the world so much love and pain resided in the house simultaneously escaped me. Sometimes we bring trouble and pain on ourselves. Other times the struggle begins in the seed. Maybe it's designed to build character. We sang that song in church, "Trials come to make you strong." Okay.

According to Exodus 3:16, the Lord (our God) told the children of Israel, "I've seen your pain." I use to question why God didn't say something like, "I allowed your suffering for a reason," or, "I took you through and allowed this painful process." It has to be difficult for a father to watch his child endure intense pain, discomfort, and suffering. When the parent is the one who created or allowed the painful circumstances in the first place, well that just adds a whole new dynamic to the situation. I finally accepted that Adam and Eve created a mess, so why not Harriett and Sylvester? Nothing new. I also accepted that God was all-knowing, so the mess came as no surprise to Him. I also concluded human and spiritual parenting are very different.

Of course, we know God did not suddenly show up for the children of Israel's wilderness experience; He was present from the beginning. He was present all the time, even in their bondage. That was a part of God's omnipresent character.

I had to go back and get understanding of who my own parents were. What were these personalities that ruled my childhood? So in search of clarity, I earnestly wanted to know the real man my dad was. I wanted to know why my mother stayed in the marriage of pain. Not ready to ask mom, I picked Daddy's brain for information. Mom eventually told me she stayed married because God never told her to get a divorce. That made sense to me but wasn't enough. I needed to know more about both of their childhoods.

I learned that Daddy was born in 1929 and accepted Christ as his personal savior in 1941. He told me that in 1997, when I fell in love with a black art print titled *Chicago Boys 1941 Sunday Suit Best.* The print reminded me of Mom and Dad as I imagined they were when the same age of these young males in

1941. When I told Daddy about the artwork, he said 1941 was special to him. It was the year he received Christ as his personal Savior and the year his grandmother died. I thought it was so cool, because I probably wouldn't have learned that little tidbit if I hadn't been so captivated by the print. This print hangs in my bedroom to this day, because there is a peace about it. It reminds me of my father.

My father grew up in Carbondale, Illinois, and had a strong, God-fearing father in Sylvester Bradley Steele Sr. That was a major blessing in the 1930s and 1940s. Grandpa Steele passed when I was ten years old. I remember him as tall, handsome, and soft-spoken. Grandma Steele was quite the opposite.

Our dad really became an alcoholic long before he joined the army. He started drinking hard liquor as a child, living in his parent's house. The damaging effects of the alcoholic disease were in place long before our family unit in Wheaton began. Alcohol drove Daddy to extremes. He was the big cowboy—fearless, expert hunter, gentle.

Daddy was discharged from the army in 1955, somehow came to the Wheaton area, and met Mom. They married in 1959. I was eighteen months old when they married.

Daddy endured much childhood pain and stress. Like other young children growing up in the 1940s and earlier, he worked hard in the fields and at home before his school day started. His education went only as far as the sixth grade, and he had a nervous breakdown around the age of sixteen. His youth was marred by beatings, where his mother would humiliate him by whipping him naked.

A broken heart, army discharge, and employment opportunities in the dry cleaning industry brought him north, to the Chicago area. Momma was attracted to the bad boy exterior, which covered a good man who knew God, loved conversation, and was capable of protecting her. Momma's consistent stories of her and Daddy's early days confirmed the truth of all those things.

Our daddy carried a dark secret that had haunted from his childhood. Our family eventually learned how that secret was the root of the internal struggle he had with loving and trusting women. He had a strong dislike for loose women.

Daddy drank away his pain and spent lots of time with others who did the same. I never understood how Daddy could sit in the driveway, in the family car, with two or three of his drinking buddies for hours, just drinking and talking. Somewhere between Daddy exiting the car bar and stumbling through the front door, he underwent a bizarre transformation that included anger. I think the sight of any one of us kids immediately made him shameful and reminded him that he was trapped. This was a weekly, almost daily, routine.

Fluctuating between wanting my daddy to die and wanting to understand what made him tick, I justified my feelings by reminding myself that he was especially mean to me. I felt he had rules that applied only to me. I secretly hated Daddy for a long time.

In my childhood, there was no clue that my daddy was in turmoil, at war within himself. He actually protected, loved, and hurt his family all at the same time. He carried each of those three things from one extreme to the other. Maybe he did the best he could.

During my childhood, my momma went to church nearly every Sunday. She was the primary church organist (we didn't call them ministers of music back then). Our mother had the most beautiful voice, and she played the piano and organ by ear. Our mom could play any kind of music. She knew how to gather us up like little chicks around the organ, and we would sing our hearts out. We had no idea that she was teaching us to focus on the positive and not the ugly. The songs she taught us ranged from silly, like the "Mr. Froggy Went a Courtin'" to gospel hymns. Mom knew harmony and would teach, play, and listen intensely to keep us on key and focused on the music. I taught my children every song Mom taught us as kids, and now, our daughter teaches her daughters these songs. Sometimes it's hysterical, but most of the time you just thank God for the blessing of passing these traditions to the next generation.

Mom trained her children to stay close to her, working puzzles and/or singing. We learned every song Mom taught the church gospel choir. Many times we would be singing and clapping when Dad came in the house, and we knew to "cool it." Other times, Daddy might already be in the house, maybe in bed, and we would be in the living room around the organ, with Mom singing. That might awaken Daddy and set him off as well. Many a fight started because we were all singing, having fun, and creating more noise in the house than Daddy could stand. It really didn't make sense to me that we should live in such craziness, because when Daddy was sober, he was upbeat, and we knew he loved us.

As far back as I can remember, there were terrible fights and cussing matches. Mom usually didn't start in with cussing but would eventually be so under attack, she would join right in and lay Daddy out with her mouth. Arguments often turned physical.

Mom worked at least two jobs for years. It's a wonder she stayed sane. She just could not get Daddy to play his part. Not the way she expected a man to. She multitasked and juggled all the time. She strove for peace, but it seemed at least once a week our home was turned upside down. Out of key. Out of order. I felt the entire county knew, and what they weren't certain of, they made up.

I often wondered why our mother never left our dad. I mean, if a man had pulled a gun on me while I was dating him, I do believe I would have run. In my opinion, Mom should have run away from Daddy fast and furious. Well, of course, I eventually asked my mom to explain that one to me. I needed to know what in the world kept her married to Daddy.

I always wondered what people knew about the real happenings within our home. Grandma Gibson knew, because she often had to swoop in to rescue us; all of us. Whenever fights broke out between Mom and Dad, one of us kids would take off running down the street, past the garden, to Grandma and Grandpa's house to get help. I don't recall Grandpa ever coming up to help at those times. Grandma would rush up and help calm Mom and Dad down. She would be very firm with Daddy, telling him to stop raising all the hell in our house and he should be ashamed of himself. It always calmed Daddy down, and he usually went to bed or took off in the car. I'm sure it was super embarrassing for Momma.

Our Gibson grandparents played a major role in our upbringing. They lived down the street, so they were always visible, watching us. Sunday mornings they picked up Sherrie and I for Sunday school and church, allowing Mom time and space to prepare the younger children and herself for church. Mom was never able to make Sunday school.

I got the biggest kick out of riding in the backseat of Grandma and Grandpa Gibson's car. Their "fussin'" was hilarious to me. Grandma would call Grandpa "son," and he called her "Lizzie." Their fussing was usually about the other one's driving. Nothing was ever crazy or out of control about their disagreements. It was just low key and funny as all get out. By the time we pulled up in front of the church (about four miles away), the argument was over. No wonder our grandparents were married for over fifty years!

Grandma Gibson prayed deliberately and continuously for her fifty-plus grandchildren. I know she did, because I heard her prayers.

When I was preschool age, my Gibson grandparents looked after me during the day. When I started half-day kindergarten, they kept me the half-day I didn't attend school. Back then you attended kindergarten in shifts, morning or afternoon.

The incest and molestation started when I was around five or six years old and continued for approximately eight years. There is a big difference between living in an inherited foolishness and sleeping in the bed of self-made foolishness. Back then I could not distinguish between the two.

I am thankful for God's grace in keeping us safe and reasonably sane through all the situations that presented themselves in our childhood years. It seems that some things happened as part of God's perfect will in my life. Looking back and searching the recollection of our story and my story, I am convinced beyond doubt that God was present through it all. When you grow up in that type of atmosphere, and you escape, it is liberating. Surely life does not have to be that stressful. But the problem is you don't have good tools; a stronghold has gripped your psyche. You tend to relive what was rehearsed in front of you. You may not realize that your norm is abnormal.

The Eye of the Storm Is no Place to Pitch Your Tent

There is a big difference in using experience as an end in itself and viewing it as a means to an end. It's probably not a good idea to remain where destruction is known to settle.

CHAPTER 4

Colossians 3:16

Let the word of Christ dwell in you richly in all
wisdom, teaching and admonishing one another
in psalms and hymns and spiritual songs, singing
with grace in your hearts to the Lord. (NKJV)

The Drill

Daddy constantly struggled with Mom's strength. As weak as
he was in everything, she was strong, and vice versa. We all
knew, from Dad on down, that Mom clung to Proverbs 22:6:
"Train up a child in the way he should go, even when he is old
he will not depart from it." She knew Dad's story like she knew
her own, and if she could come back to her senses, find her way
back to her spirituality, and stay on track, certainly Dad—and
anyone else for that matter—could do so as well. Mom stood
firm in her faith that Dad would be healed from the alcohol and
return to a right relationship with the Lord. She wanted more
than anything for him to come back to church with her where
they could serve God together. She would get tiny glimpses of
his wanting to reconnect with his spirituality, but the problem
was it always seemed to come on the tail end of inebriation.

Our father struggled with his faith. When Daddy was behaving as the "happy drunk," he always wanted to sing. Dad had a wonderful, strong, full voice, but he sang loudly, really loudly. There was always the same lineup of songs he wanted Momma to play so he could sing. So Mom would sit at the organ and play. I would watch her face a lot. She didn't always want to play for Daddy, because she was tired, and he was drunk. If she wasn't physically tired, I'm certain she was mentally exhausted. I am sure that for Mom to sit at that organ and listen to Daddy sing gospel songs as loud as he could, with heavily liquored breath, felt like a slap to her face. Sometimes Mom let her frustration show, but that scenario never ended well. A big argument would ensue. Then there were times when Dad would sing until tears came to his eyes, and he would break down and have to go to bed to sleep it off.

Daddy's ritual would tug at your heart. There were times when his drinking buddies joined him. For some reason, their behavior was both sad and comical. Daddy and his friends would get out of the car, where they had been sitting in the driveway for hours and drinking, and then come in the house, totally wasted, and beg Mom to play the organ. Three or four of them would sing, loudly, doo-wopping and hollering to the point where they totally annihilated the gospel songs and pushed Mom beyond her patience. We kids would watch and laugh. It was like an Eddie Murphy comedy routine, except his routines remain funny. These memories ceased to be comical many years ago, because these were real people, real men. They were broken men who were obviously hurting deep inside. I think they were all beautiful men who had experienced some intense pain in their lives and woke up one morning inside of a liquor bottle, drowning in their personal failures.

This was the drill my father rehearsed—in front of all us children—over and over again. I'm convinced it affected each of us children in ways we never realized until we were adults with children of our own. None of us wanted to repeat this craziness with our own families.

There is a saying, "Whatever is in the well will come up in the bucket." I think I will agree with the statement. Once I got old enough to really watch and listen with both my eyes and heart, I realized Mom and Dad had the same thing in their wells. You would just have to draw a little deeper to pull the good up from Daddy's well.

Both Momma and Daddy knew the Word of God, they both were raised in the church, and they both had accepted Christ at a young age. They both had endured some serious pain by the time they reached age twenty, and they both had lost some children along the way. They both had suffered previous marriages. Mom had suffered a lot of pain through the disdain of her father, and Dad had suffered at the hands of his mother. Both Mom and Dad had beautiful voices and held the music in their souls.

The difference was Mom had been reconciled to her God sometime around 1962. Her mind was made up, and she was serious about her redemption. Dad, on the other hand, had also lost his way, but it would be twenty years before he would make a conscious decision to stop wallowing in the mud and trust God completely. In many ways, the fact that Mom had recovered and had more of an education to fall back on didn't help matters one bit.

Every day of my childhood was marked by fear. As I would walk home from grade school through high school, it did not matter which corner I came around—Hill Avenue to Wood

Street, or Avery to Wood Street—I feared I would see the worst in front of our house. Police cars or an ambulance would signal that someone was dead. The car in the driveway would mean Daddy and his buddies were drinking early.

I don't recount this to lay blame. I had to relive so much of it in my mind to understand that all things work together in our lives to establish who we are, what we have become, and what was simply beyond our control. Things happen that we have no control over, and they provide real matter that impacts us whether we like it or not. It is a blessing to look back and celebrate the goodness of God. In reflecting on life at 316 Wood Street, I see the hand of God, if for no other reason, because no one died. Not physically anyway.

If it had not been for Mom's gift of music, things would have been a lot worse. If she had not been committed to passing on the songs and her faith to us kids, we would have had no hope. I am forever thankful for the mother we had.

In 1968, it was very common to hear "fire and brimstone" preaching. Frightened children occupied many a mourners' bench. We didn't have a mourners' bench at Second Baptist back then, but we had some serious preaching about hell and choosing God or Satan. The first time I was baptized, at ten years old, the decision was probably driven by fear. I was a sinner, and the recurring dreams of God cracking the sky and the world ending gave me a sense of an imminent end of the world! I needed to be saved, so one revival weeknight (probably a Friday night, because I recall struggling all week long), I got saved.

Eventually, Sherrie got talked into going up the aisle and accepting Christ with me. Over the years, I've gotten the biggest chuckle out of this scene, wondering how long Sherrie and I sat there dialoguing before coming to the conclusion that we could, indeed, make the journey from our bench to shake the pastor's hand. We did it together! Then we were baptized on a Sunday morning. I don't know about Sherrie, but I was scared to death of going into that baptismal pool. I just knew I was going to drown. Thank God we both made it. I looked at my hands, and they did not look new. My feet didn't either. My sinning definitely didn't stop. But I believed I was saved. So now this contradiction of expectancy added to the frustration. Was I going to lose my salvation? Why couldn't I stop sinning? I kept having those little talks with Jesus, but I wasn't getting anything back but guilt and condemnation. The reply messaging was coming from my head, not my heart. I was ten years old, and this was way too heavy a load to carry and comprehend.

In the mix of all those questions I lived in fear every day that something terrible would happen in our home because of the fussing and fighting. It wasn't until many years later, in the navy, that I learned how I braced my body, practically 24/7 to prepare for fright or flight. I was controlled by stress.

Inspect Your Well

Whatever is in the well will be drawn up in the bucket.

Chapter 5

Isaiah 3:16

The LORD says "Beautiful Zion is haughty: craning her elegant neck, flirting with her eyes, walking with dainty steps, tinkling her ankle bracelets." (NLT)

Puffed Up: a.k.a. Bad Judgment

The summer of 1973 was a significant turning point in my teenage life. I was fifteen years old. I can't begin to explain how puppy love becomes a crush, becomes infatuation, becomes an all-out leave of your senses, but that pretty much wraps up the sequence of events leading to my first marriage.

Everyone believed I was mature for my age, but I was gullible just the same. The fact of the matter was I was promiscuous and overconfident, acting out of conditioning. I could put up a good show, but inside, I was split in two, like two people altogether, fearful and unwise, grownup and childlike. One person wanted to live as a Christian, honest and free to have fun and trust people. The other personality was always fearful, insecure, and frigid from the inside out. The one soul searched daily for avenues of escape from home.

My immaturity repeatedly showed in the bad choices I made, especially in intimate relationships.

In retrospect, it is easier to just be honest about it all. How a fifteen-year-old girl can pull off a relationship with a young man six years her senior deserves some looking into.

Never the type of young lady to be called over the top, showy, confident, or risqué, I concluded I was more like the girl next door. Watching television, I concluded that males were attracted to the girl next door. Now I know I had learned very early to flirt with clean conversation. There's no better way to put it. At the risk of being too open, I have to say it took me over thirty years to learn this aspect of my personality and to see that it, too, was a result of learned behavior. What a mess I created.

So at fifteen I was flirting with my big brother's best friend. He was a young man six years my senior. In truth, it was a strange dance of predator and pursuer. He was a twenty-one-year-old male, and I was a flirtatious young girl, throwing myself at him. It is the truth of what I did. Looking back, I would understand that this relationship was also a "safe," well-calculated, conscious move on my part. And even though the reality of that statement seems a little unfair, it's honest. I knew what I was doing, but I didn't understand that my actions were just part of the struggle, the tug-of-war that had gone on inside me since about the age of five. I do not believe the five-year relationship was a coincidence. It was a part of my life that had to be. I believe that. I just happened to be sitting on my grandparents' front porch one summer day in June 1973, and he just happened to be visiting. He just happened to come by the very next day, and I just happened to be waiting for it to happen.

❤ *Sylvia Steele-Dunn*

My father confronted us about the relationship, but it seemed so genuine that he didn't bother to come against it. My mother would later tell me that she never stopped it, because she thought I conducted myself in a mature manner, and if she tried to stop me, it would only provoke me to pursue the relationship even more.

So for three years, off and on, I dated this young man, and six months after my high school graduation, we married. By the time I turned twenty, I was beyond needing a divorce. As a matter of fact, that was just what the doctor ordered. Hospitalized for severe migraine headaches in 1978, the psychiatrist said, "You don't need a doctor. You need a divorce."

One of the most significant things I learned about myself is that major decisions, those that require the head and heart to be in agreement, were not easy for me. I am the type of person who could easily get stuck in self-destructive behavior mode. Despite my intolerance for physical or emotional beat downs, I wrestled with the divorce decision nearly a full year. Then one day at work I happened to read something that was totally out of character for me: the horoscopes. That morning Pisces read: "Today is the day to take care of that legal paperwork." I immediately called my lawyer, Phil Sullivan. "Phil, file the papers." Phil pulled the papers he had filed away, awaiting my call to move ahead. So it was full steam ahead. Within a few months, we were divorced.

I was too young for marriage, and this phase of my life was the catalyst for leaving home and really forge my own life away from 316 Wood Street. I'm okay with all the friendships that were developed over all the crazy years. But I'm more grateful for the understanding that I was really torn between two paths and personalities. One path (or personality) was a by-product of early childhood molestation and a desire to be accepted. This path ultimately would lead to dozens of healthy and unhealthy relationships. The second, more acceptable, path (or personality) is one that is often mistaken for being stuck-up but is actually a confidence and comfort in knowing I have come through so much with the help of the Lord, and my God loves me enough to supply my needs and be the center of my joy. That path required a daily confidence boost. I had to remind myself that I had paid a price to secure my self-confidence.

More than anything, I learned much about forgiveness from a failed marriage. I learned to forgive myself and be honest about times of being a victim and times of being part of the problem. I learned what I would not, could not, tolerate in a marriage. I learned that you forgive someone for yourself. You have to forgive in order to release yourself from an emotional prison. I learned that hate is not the opposite of love but is love on furious steroids.

Above all I learned that just like those Israelites, even if I failed at certain efforts, as long as there was God-given breath, blood, and spirit, He was actively pulling for my success in all areas.

Who Is in Control?

If God is Alpha and Omega,
then He alone sets the flight plan
and sets the controls.

CHAPTER 6

Joshua 3:16

The water above that point began backing up a great
distance away at a town called Adam, which is near
Zarethan. And the water below that point flowed on to
the Dead Sea until the riverbed was dry. Then all the
people crossed over near the town of Jericho. (NLT)

Crossing Over

Sometime around my eighteenth birthday, I planned a grownup, high-profile escape. It was doomed for failure from the
start. The first clue came during my wedding on September
25, 1976 (three months after high school graduation). It hit me
as Daddy walked me down the aisle. Daddy smelled of alcohol,
and I was asking and answering myself, *Is it too late to call this
off? Yeah, it's too late.* When you escape, you take yourself with
you … who knew?

I thought a stable and respectable escape route had been
chosen, but craziness followed. It was in my blood and character.
I was wired for repeats.

Following a short-lived marriage, I once again planned an
acceptable escape to maintain some sort of sanity. This time it

was all about me. Everything would be left behind. I joined the navy in March of 1979. I would soon understand that dysfunctional was a new normal. Dysfunctional families were commonplace. People just learned to keep their mess hidden.

Early in the morning of June 27, 1979, the navy recruiter picked me up from 316 Wood Street, and I was off for the first time—really me against the world. Within hours, I was in route to basic training in Orlando, Florida. I was scared to death, yet deep inside, there was a belief that things would be all right.

I had been baptized for the second time about a month prior to leaving for basic training. My assurance was high that I carried my faith with me, and it served me well. There was a certainty that I was on the right path. I left my parents' home for the second time since turning eighteen. I knew it was an escape route, but this time it wasn't all my own creation, and the God I believed in and prayed to was where I had to put my trust.

I like Joshua 3:14, which says, "So the people left their camp to cross the Jordan, and the priests who were carrying the Ark of the Covenant went ahead of them."(NLT). So this is the book of Joshua, six books into the Old Testament, and once again, God was proving himself to the children of Israel. The people were crossing over on dry ground. Reading the Old Testament, you find over and over how these chosen people had to relearn lessons and be delivered or saved by their God.

I felt like those biblical children of Israel. The Lord had made a way of escape, and I was walking it out. This time I was leaving my parents' home at 316 wrapped in the comfort that the Lord would make a way for me, walk with me, and go ahead of me. That is the essence of what I believed from that day forward. This time I was truly crossing over. My goal was also to leave Egypt behind.

Every new and difficult navy experience, starting with boot camp, challenged my entire being. Yet I learned if I kept my composure, even the biggest fears would fade. Boot camp exercised mind, muscle, and faith.

Foremost, I was a nonswimmer, and that proved to be an overwhelming challenge. The recruiter showed me the video of recruits jumping off the diving board to help prepare me for the impending shock. It did not phase me one way or another. There was a confidence that I could get to boot camp and have some help figuring it out. Once I got to Orlando, however, the diving board intimidated and scared me to death.

The fear of drowning began in my early teens, when a young man took me out into the deep end of a swimming pool and left me there. I couldn't swim, so you can imagine what happened, short of drowning. So climbing the ladder to the top of that diving board was one of the most fearful walks I've ever taken. When I arrived at the top, I froze. I heard the whistle blow but could not jump. After I missed the jump signal the second time, the training petty officer told me if I didn't jump this next time, he was climbing the ladder and pushing me in. That would have been a disaster for sure. I jumped. And they had to fish me out of the water with a pole. How embarrassing. That evening I asked a group of girls to huddle around, and we prayed about this diving board thing.

The next morning when the training unit had to jump from the high dive, I walked out to the pool. I happened to glance down and discovered a little, blue, plastic smiley face. It made me smile, so I picked it up and tucked it into my swimsuit. I felt it was a gift, and even though I believed I would never dive and swim, there was confidence I could dive and float. I was not afraid.

Basic training was an intense eight weeks of calling on and drawing from every ounce of strength I had. My company commanders chose me as a training unit section leader. I was even scared of that challenge initially. I think there were eight or ten girls in each section. Some of these girls looked a little ruthless, and I was accustomed to steering clear of aggressive women. I didn't realize I was turning into quite an aggressive little sister myself. I was also learning how to defend myself and be assertive. I liked that part.

Every training day was exhausting. During evening chores, like mopping and waxing the decks or cleaning the heads, I would teach my section gospel songs. A few of the girls pulled me aside later and told me how much it meant to them. All I knew was what Mom had instilled in us; during stressful times, accentuate the positive and draw from inner strength. Boot camp proved to be one of the best experiences of my entire life.

When basic training was over, I felt like a new person. I had new and very rough calluses on my feet and rough knees from scrubbing floors and kneeling to tile and praying by my rack each night. My fear of large bodies of water was a little diminished. I could float and was darn proud of it. The Lord didn't part the water for me to walk across. He didn't need to. It was important that I stay in the water, not walk on dry land. He made a way for me by showing up in the form of a smiley face and calming my fears long enough for me to pass the diving board and float tests. My God supplied what I needed to survive the tests. I can't swim to this day! But I can float forever for survival and enjoyment.

At the conclusion of basic training, I was meritoriously promoted to the next rank. The blessing of that promotion showed me to always pray my way through and accept leadership challenges knowing I wasn't going to be the best at everything. I was okay with that. I had crossed over!

During my first duty assignment in San Diego, I realized how sheltered, naïve, and damaged I really was. It was no secret—I allowed my feelings of hope for my sisters and brothers to go a little overboard at times. The problem seemed to be that no matter how old we got, I always felt like the big sister, responsible for shooting off at the mouth to help. After all, this is what Mom drilled into me so many times as a child. "You are the oldest!" Good grief, I couldn't keep myself in line when we were growing up. How in the world? Maybe it happened once I became an adult and felt I had overcome so many things. My family had no idea what I had really been through.

After arriving in San Diego in November 1979, I became consumed with worry for my family in Illinois. Mom would tell me about certain ones running amuck, adding stress on her and Dad. I worried even more for my family, and that caused friction between younger siblings and myself that lasted many years. Somehow, I could not mind my own business. For my baby sister, I would replay what she told me a few years earlier. "I'm not gonna make the mistakes you guys made. I'm gonna learn from you all's mistakes," she told me. It seemed from that point on, and as situations would come and go, I would just shake my head and think, *Learn from our mistakes, huh?*

In July 2011, I discovered a letter in my mother's Carbondale home. I had written it to my father on April 5, 1980, while stationed in San Diego. Finding that letter was like a gift from my father's spirit. I had long forgotten writing the letter, and on rereading, it became clear it had marked a turning point in the relationship I enjoyed with my father for many years prior to his death. I wrote to my father, opening up to him about how I really felt about him. I recalled a conversation around 1990, when Daddy told me that the Lord had blessed me with a gift of healing. I recall many things by association, where I was at the time or how I responded to something. I remember my response to Dad's statement was, "Yeah, right." But now I understand.

The letter brings me to tears each time I read it. It was six pages and the cover page simply read:

DADDY—BEFORE YOU GET ANGRY

READ MY *ENTIRE* LETTER.

LOVE YOU MUCH—SYLVIA

The letter read exactly this way.

April 5, 1980

Dear Daddy,

How are you? I realize that is an open and highly debatable question.

I have been thinking about writing you a very serious letter for a long time now. First of all let me begin by apologize to you for my outburst of laughter when I heard the news about Grandma

Steele. When momma told me she did not highlight the seriousness of the situation. I still do not understand fully. So I'll take it that she could be in a lot of trouble. For well over a year now I've been wanting to discuss some issues with you. As you may very well know I do not understand you, although I have tried.

One particular subject has a lot to do with my divorce. I do not recall exactly when this one incident happened but Keith so rudely brought it to my attention that you had told him about some of your personal business. Right in the middle of one of our fights he made the statement that you were correct when you told him I was a lot like my mother. He said you told him that momma had an abortion a long time ago. This child supposedly was between Sherrie and Brad or Brad and Robert, I don't recall. All I know is this … If the story is true you need to take a good look at yourself. By now you should know that what happens between you and momma is your business. Keith should never have been told that … you should learn something daddy. Momma does not profess to have been perfect all her life; you get angry because she goes to church so much. I'm glad she does because it keeps her from losing her mind. If it weren't for her our family would've been shot to hell a long time ago. I don't and never have judged either of you for what you've done in your pasts. As your daughter and as a person it's not my place to. I'm glad you never lied to us. We all have known who our full brothers and sisters are as well as those by previous marriages or mishaps.

I remember so many times when I was young and you and momma would fight and argue. I hated it. And I remember the way you would call it to our attention that mom had kids that were/are illegitimate. I say so damn what! Isn't there a God out there somewhere who says "I forgive"?

People tell me I worry about my family too much. This is true. I love my family. You guys are all I have. It really hurts to see so many crazy things going on at home.

Since January I have been saving money so that when I come home in June I could buy a car (because they're cheaper at home) and drive back to California. Now I'm finding out not only is the Navy screwing up on sending my money but momma had had to use it on occasions to pay bills and just plain make ends meet. I've never been so mad since I've been in the Navy. Tell me something, do you plan on doing something about this? I'm speaking of something such as getting a job and being the man.

Daddy it takes more than drinking and fixing a leaky pipe every now and then. And it sure takes more than being a grouch.

I remember once when I was in Mississippi you told me to send you some money. I felt like hanging up on you. Instead I overlooked it and then later I cried. Why I cried I don't know.

Since I've been away from home mom has always taken time out to write me. I see her exhaustion between the lines. I can picture her trying to make ends meet, and I wonder what your role is. I'm sure you think I've got a lot of nerve. And I do. If you can't accept me as a whole person, no longer a child—out here trying to make it—well then that's cool. It won't change who I am, how I came to be and my purpose.

Daddy I love you so much it hurts. The hurt is because I also dislike your ways. You've been at semi stand still since Aunt Bea died. It hurt me too. Aunt Bea is the only one of my aunt who wrote me since last June when I came in the service. But life goes on. I listen to you all tell me about the many people who are passing away. Sounds like a communicable disease and it is. Don't die with those people daddy. The Bible says "Let the dead bury the dead" Remember, God is not dead! And if you are you're not only worthless but wasting living space at home.

After I got my divorce it took a long time for me to be at peace with myself. I want to be at peace with you also.

Sometimes I sit around with some of the other sisters who are in the Navy. We talk about our childhoods. It's the same all over. All we ask from our parents is love and guidance. We seem to make our mistakes early in life also as our parents may or may not have done. But the story always repeats itself. "Girl, you should see my father"—"You wouldn't want to see my father"—"I remember so much when I was little of my father beating up my mother"—"My father left us when we were just babies"—it goes on and on.

I don't compare because you raised us, you helped also. But you hurt so much. I know you and mom can't get along all the time but how about being partners some of the time.

I feel better now. I've gotten this off my chest. Hope this letter makes it to the mailbox.

One last thing—I don't know when I'll be home because I don't know if I'll be able to afford it, but when I do come home don't act as though you never received this letter.

I love you and momma,

God bless,

Sissy

P.S. I hope you will write me.

Today when people remind me of where I come from, I say, *"You're right."* But I remind myself that I put in the work of learning who my father really was, and I reached out to him to repair the breach. I communicated both love and concern for him. Most important, I know he heard my heart, because we became the very best of friends. Once Dad told me our relationship was threefold. He said he thanked God that I was his daughter, friend, and sister in Christ. What more could I ask for? Nothing. By the time Daddy passed on to glory, there was nothing missing from our relationship, and nothing was left undone. My relationship with my father had truly come full circle.

The Lord truly saw the misery suffered in Egypt (316 Wood), and He remains faithful and concerned. I had to leave my Egypt.

Alcoholism, incest, rejection, molestation are all deep-rooted, destructive spirits that wreak havoc in families for generations. Why consider these spirits? Because they are seductive and dangerously deceptive. These types of spirits follow their assignments and transfer—well. Family is an organism. It is a unit where love, trust, hope, and growth are meant to exist. It is a place where the children should feel safe. It is not a place to sleep through one another's pain.

Not only are alcoholism and rejection formidable forces that must be addressed and destroyed, they are mental strongholds. What is a stronghold? In short, strongholds are manifested, fortified thoughts. Love, forgiveness, prayer, fasting, and/or confrontation can break a stronghold. We have to seek the right mix. Communication is key. Love must be communicated. Forgiveness must be communicated. Confrontation can be a useful form of communication if done in love. Your goal, if you are operating in love, is to annihilate/crush the stronghold, not the person. The person is a child of God the Creator, who gave it spirit, breath, and life. I believe we should strive to convey, "I am concerned about you," rather than, "I am sickened by you."

Look Up!

It just not healthy to live defeated. Lift your spirit.

CHAPTER 7

James 3:16

For where jealousy and selfish ambition exist, there is disorder and every evil thing.

Tore Up, Basement Up

Growing up in Wheaton, Illinois, I was afforded many visits to the Wheaton College campus. Ultimately, the Billy Graham ministry blessed our family. Of course, Reverend Billy Graham did not know us personally, but he inadvertently blessed us just the same.

It was the salvation preaching of the Reverend Billy Graham that really drew me as a child to seriously make the initial decision to give my heart to the Lord. Even before I made the decision to be baptized, our grandmother Gibson took us Billy Graham crusades in Chicago.

In 1977, Billy Graham indirectly impacted our family at 316 Wood Street when our parents were blessed with a house. The Billy Graham Center at Wheaton College was scheduled to begin groundbreaking and building, but first, five houses had to be removed from the targeted site on College Avenue.

Mom learned that Wheaton College planned to sell the

houses for one dollar, but the buyer had to incur costs of moving the homes from their current location to anywhere necessary. I wasn't aware of the entire procedure, but in the end, my mom and my soon to be ex-husband acquired two of the houses up for grabs.

I never lived a single day in the house my ex-husband got, because I informed my divorce lawyer my soon to be ex-husband could have the house, because I just wanted my sanity! My lawyer tried to convince me otherwise, but I was firm. I still have no idea what I walked away from, but I do know I have never regretted my decision.

The house my parents obtained was a whole other story entirely. The house was a divine blessing, because their home was about to cave in, literally. From inside the house you would never know it, but if you went into the basement and looked closely, you would see major cracks in the foundation. Our Gibson grandparents laid the original foundation. Basically, my parents had not put any significant work or improvement into the house at 316 Wood Street. I recall Mom painting and wallpapering, but I haven't a single recollection of my father ever doing anything significant to enhance the three-bedroom house they rented from Mom's parents.

If my mom had not had the sense to go for this opportunity, and the smarts to see the project through, there is no telling what would have become of that old house at 316 Wood Street.

Our old house was demolished and replaced by a big, two-story house. A new foundation was poured, and the College Avenue home was moved onto the same soil that was once owned by our grandparents. Our mother oversaw the entire project.

I still have pictures from the day our old house was bulldozed.

I was working for DuPage County at the time and took a few hours off to go watch the old house being torn down. Although I no longer lived at that address with my parents, it was quite moving. It was bittersweet. That house was filled with so many intense good and bad memories.

The contractor that oversaw the house moving was Peter "Pete" Frieson. He was a well-known, expert structure mover. How Mom was able to get him, I do not know. But I can guess that someone from the county helped her contact this guy. Mom said this Pete Frieson was known for being the best. He was an immigrant from the Ukraine and lived in the Chicago area.

From my position, it seemed Dad was jealous of Mom, and that is how I rationalized Daddy's need to control something, no matter how simple or bizarre. The truth was that Mom was highly respected and greatly appreciated in the county. Mom had worked for DuPage County for over twenty years and finally retired in 1993. Mom was greatly liked. People often showed their appreciation to her on Christmas and Valentine's Day. At Christmas, a few women Mom worked with would buy us kids Christmas presents, and Mom would get boxes of candy from the board members she supported. The best treat of all was when the mysterious packages of steaks were delivered about a week before Christmas. I never knew who sent the filet mignons, but I know I ate my share of them.

The demolition of the first house on 316 Wood Street was one of those situations where Mom pulled all her strength together to make something positive happen, with or without Daddy.

Momma lived in that house as a child. Then when her parents purchased their new home down the street, at 1518 Hill

Avenue, my mom and a few of her sisters—young women in their early twenties—stayed in the house at 316 Wood Street.

So in the beginning, way back in the 1950s, that house at 316 Wood Street was available for the children born to Hollis and Elizabeth Gibson to live in as need arose. As with many families, the purpose changed over time, and circumstances dictated modification of the original plan. My mother is the last of her siblings to reside in that house.

There was a time when each of my mother's older sisters lived in the house at 316 Wood Street. Eventually, after my parents returned from Freeport Illinois, and after a couple of years of living in my grandparents' basement at 1518 Hill Avenue, my parents moved us into the house at 316 Wood Street. My mom wasn't able to tell me what year we moved into 316 Wood Street, but I believe it was around 1962 or 1963, before I started elementary school.

From my earliest recollection, my mother worked in our home as a beautician and outside of the house doing full-time secretarial work. During those years, Mom was so busy working, having babies, and putting up with our father's shenanigans that she wasn't able to keep up with everything we kids were doing. I felt she was especially unaware of things that were going on in my life. I think Mom felt she had it covered, because we spent time in school, church, and visiting neighbors, but the truth is there was a lot of time that I spent getting into trouble. My trouble didn't bring problems for the family as much as it brought consequences for me personally.

I don't know when it started exactly—the molestation, the incest, the out-of-control sexual behavior—but it had to have started extremely early, because it was already going on when I was five and six years old.

As early as second grade, I learned to escape the house. I would visit my grandparents for hours and walk the streets, visiting elderly people in the neighborhood. The neighborhood was safe, and everybody knew everybody, so you weren't concerned with safety. I started escaping past the neighborhood around third grade, visiting friends from school, playing, and getting involved in activities that gave me excuses to delay the return home. Many times, parents of the kids I played with would bring me home. I probably got on their nerves, but no one ever let on. People treated me nicely, often asking me to stay for dinner or go with them to different church activities. I became actively involved in groups like Brownies, Girl Scouts, and Pioneer Girls, Jet Cadets, anything that was safe. These activities provided great escapes. These activities also afforded me opportunities to see how other people lived and to see the "appearance" of normalcy.

Somewhere between all the positive activities, many times I would find myself alone in my grandparents' basement with older male cousins. Specifically, there were two male cousins who were five and six years older than me, and these were the two "relationships" that were the most damaging to my psyche. As I got a little older, I would go down in that basement, looking for the petting and sexual contact from my older cousins. This went on for years, and eventually I realized, somewhere around sixth grade, that I could get pregnant by a cousin. It was worse than that actually. My cousins would talk bad about me, and my reputation was very bad, especially among other females. In grade school, I had very few friends. On top of it all, I hated home, mostly because I was embarrassed by my father.

When the house was torn down, I was relieved. That house was crazy. Even the basement held horrible memories for me.

The basement was dingy, disorderly. Approximately half the basement floor was a strangely configured and broken slab of concrete, while the other half was dirt and gravel. It was a place where children played, experimented, were molested, and were promiscuous. To me, that basement just felt evil. I can't recollect a single good thing that happened in that basement, or any other basement for that matter.

Relationships

My internal relationship with the Father is reflected in my external dealings with my fellow man.

CHAPTER 8

Hebrews 3:16

And who was it who rebelled against God,
even though they heard his voice? Wasn't it the
people Moses led out of Egypt? (NLT)

Rebellious Ways

The year 1986 was tough from beginning to end. In my search to find me, I had to go back and pause a long time in 1986 because midyear I had became stuck on the question, Where do you store tainted memories? Should we even store tainted memories? Who had the answer? I sure didn't.

With all my heart I had loved my big brother Ted as for long as I could remember. He graduated from Wheaton Central High School two years before I got there, but he had been so well known that kids would stop me and ask, "Are you Ted Steele's little sister?" I was so proud to respond yes. But by that time, Ted was discovering he was not really Ted Steele but Ted Gibson according to his birth certificate. Although Daddy had raised him from three years old, his name had never been legally changed to Steele.

To make matters worse, Ted discovered his birthday had

been celebrated on the wrong day all of his life. Our mother must have been stressed out when Ted was born. Over eighteen years of celebrating your birthday on the wrong date! Wow.

At any rate, I looked up to Ted, literally, all my life. When I started grade school, Ted was responsible for walking me to and from school. Children attended kindergarten only half a day, and I was assigned to the morning session. Mornings were especially cold in the winter months, but Ted made sure I did not freeze to death. We had a system, because Ted was in the sixth grade and would often take his time hanging with his friends, I received clear direction to go to the janitor's room and wait there for him to pick me up. Mr. Jackson and Mr. Robinson, two wonderful men from the neighborhood, kept an eye on me and made me feel right comfortable in the boiler room. One of them would always be in the boiler room when I arrived. I remember looking all around that boiler room, just checking out my surroundings. I loved heat, so that room was very comfortable to me. I remember that the three of them—Ted, Mr. Jackson, and Mr. Robinson—made me feel very special.

Ted was the second of three children Mom birthed prior to meeting Daddy in 1957. Ted was the only one of those children that Mom actually raised. So Ted grew up as the oldest child in our house, which means our dad raised Ted. Growing up with Ted as big brother was all right with me, because he was "cool" and had a tendency to boldly go where no one had gone before.

When I became a teenager, I would sit in the boys' bedroom or the bathroom, and Ted would talk a lot, educating me on what was going on in the world at large, according to him. I always learned something from him. For example, he was the one who had told me that we had an older sister named Pandora and that Timothy was not our uncle but our brother. Whatever questions I had, Ted was more than happy to accommodate. However, I was always seeking facts, so I almost always went to Mom for confirmation or clarification.

When Ted was getting ready to go hang out at night, I would often hang around, talking to him and watching how he manicured his afro. He would go on and on about school, girls, Daddy, black history, all sorts of stuff. He talked a lot while he washed up, and I asked a lot of questions. I always looked at him closely. Ted had these handsome, huge, brown eyes. I loved Ted's eyes, and sometimes when he slept, I would creep up on him and stare into his eyes to see if he would move. He slept with his eyes half open, so you really weren't sure if he was sleep or awake. He was usually asleep.

Ted was the most fun when he was in high school. He would wrestle the five of us younger kids around the living room floor and tickle us until our stomachs ached from the pain of his strong hands digging in our bellies. He was totally hysterical when he chased us around the house with his eyelids turned inside out, saying, "Kiss me … kiss me!" Of course, he would often grow tired of us as well. More than once he threatened to feed us chocolate laxatives if we didn't stop begging for his candy bars. Our big brother was a lot of fun, but it seems the more adult he became, the stranger and more distant he became—as far as I was concerned. He started talking a lot about revolution, being black, and raising a clinched fist.

I didn't realize it at the time, but our big brother was beginning to experiment with hard drugs. It soon became evident in the way he became combative and disrespectful toward our dad. He would push it a little further with Mom, but ways always respectful toward Momma.

One night I was coming into the house and concluded that I was alone in the house. The front door opened straight into the living room, and from that point, you could scan the kitchen, dining room, and a hallway that led to the three bedrooms. After going to the bathroom, I was certain no one else was in the house. Ted could have been in his bedroom the entire time or come in at some unknown point to me. I'm not sure, but it was only a short time before I knew without a doubt I had not been in the house alone as I thought. Mom and the rest of the kids arrived, and we were all watching TV or whatever.

Then came the blood-curdling screams that scared the heck out of all of us. Ted was in his bedroom, screaming "Ma-ma! Ma-ma! Ma-ma!"

I recall at some point Mom was on the phone, talking to someone about Ted overdosing on something called "goofballs" mixed with alcohol. Mom said, "Well, I guess my son decided to take a trip," in the beginning of the conversation, and it was so obvious that Mom had no clue what Ted had actually experienced. She was trying her best to get some help without sounding clueless. Ted did eventually tell Mom where he had been earlier that evening and what he had done. I never knew exactly.

My brother called me into his bedroom later that night, desperate to tell me the story of what happened after he had taken the pills earlier that evening. He told me he died. He was hit by a train and died. He actually stood over his body while a bunch of people gathered around. Believe him: he died. Then he heard God's voice tell him he was going to be given another chance. He was nothing but serious. He asked, "You believe me, don't you?"

I told him, "I believe you." He continued to insist that somebody had to believe him. It was his truth. *Somebody has to believe him,* I thought. He wouldn't deliberately lie to me. He had actually died earlier that evening, and God gave him a second chance. I really wanted to believe him, but deep down, I didn't. Love for my big brother was enormous, more than I can express, and there was never a reason not to believe in him.

Eventually, I matured and accepted the inevitable: big brother was just as human as the rest of us. Like all the rest of us who ever lived at 316 Wood Street, he had a rebellious nature and his own demons to fight.

After many serious fights and arguments with Mom and Dad, Ted was kicked out of the house. He began challenging beliefs and teachings at the core of Mom's heart.

Ted and I remained close. He would sometimes stop by the house while our parents were at work and take me riding with him. I hated it when he eventually left for the army.

Good memories became tainted by information that came to light after he passed in February of 1986. Today, those memories are cherished. Love allows me to keep the good. It is a choice. To not allow love to do its perfect work would be rebellious on my part. God gave me my big brother, and I love and miss him still.

Is It 'Cause of U I'm Sinnin'?

Now I gotta go back,
All the way back, back down them stairs.
Can't go down them stairs no more.
Will die if I keep going down them stairs,
No!
Gotta run up,
Run up and grab that preacher's hand.
Is it cuz of you?
I'm kinda foggy on it.
Started out running down, playing round,
up and down on the ground.
Wanna play?
No!
Dirt, stinky clothes smashed upside my face.
People talkin', talkin', justa talkin'.
Don't wanna stay and play.
Don't trust you anyway.
No!
Gotta get up from down here.
Gotta get back up those stairs.
There is safety,
But it's not down here.
It's up those stairs!
Gotta get up and
stay up …
for me.

CHAPTER 9

1 John 3:16

We know what real love is because Jesus gave up
his life for us. So we also ought to give up our
lives for our brothers and sisters. (NLT)

Count the Costs

On February 10, 1986, I received the call that my big brother,
Ted, had passed.

The last time I saw my big brother was in the summer of
1985, while I was home on leave. Ted was on dialysis then, and
he looked so worn that I knew I would not see him alive again.
It is the type of feeling that hits you in the gut, and you fight it
with your brain to prevent it from coming out of your mouth.
In my heart, I knew it was coming—soon. While I was home,
we spent some time together. I took him to dialysis at Central
DuPage Hospital, and afterward, he and I had lunch.

It was not a good time for my husband to get away, so I
flew home with our fourteen-month-old baby girl. It was a
conscious decision to take the baby. If I had to take care of my
child, I knew I would not break down and fall apart during the
funeral. As life would have it, my daughter would eventually

prove over and over again to be a child I could lean on and draw strength from. Somehow that doesn't seem fair, the parent leaning on the child, but I have come to understand God built her like that. Reciprocation is good.

The flight from Norfolk, Virginia, to Chicago O'Hare was so tough. Jeanine was an easy baby to travel with, but I kept crying, feeling sorry for myself because I had to go home with just her and myself. My brother Tim picked us up from the airport and filled me in on the details of Ted's last few months and passing. It was tough listening to Tim talk about Ted's struggle with dialysis and continued drug use. Ted had apparently continued to do drugs to cope with the pain in his body and life. It just seemed to me to be a terribly tragic end to the life of someone I loved so dearly and who had so much talent.

It was a closed casket wake and funeral. Apparently my big brother died in front of a space heater, so his body was badly decomposed. I never got complete understanding of how it all happened. In reality, I'm pretty sure I never wanted to know, so the absence of detail was fine with me.

It was a bitterly cold winter day when we went to the cemetery. We were all still terribly shaken, but no one seemed to be as affected as much as our baby sister, Cindy. Cindy was a wreck like I had never witnessed before. At the grave Cindy broke down, crying so hard it took two or three people to get her together and pull her away from the gravesite. I couldn't help but think her actions were a little extreme. I had no idea they were to close. Ted's wife didn't break down this way, our mother didn't, and I didn't, so why did Cindy?

It would be nearly a year before the truth of what Cindy had experienced that day came out. Cindy finally opened up to the sisters. On the phone she asked, "Don't you remember all the times I would beg you and Sherrie to take me with you when you left the house?" I vaguely remembered, but it was probably true. We were older than she by five and six years, so she couldn't hang out with us. The more I thought about it, the more all kinds of things came to me. How Cindy would indeed beg to go with us, and recollections and visions of our big brother holding Cindy's hand and leading her through the house were also intact in my mind. She told me how our big brother had molested her many times, making her do terrible things. She told me how he gave her money to keep her quiet.

If what Cindy said were true, it brought a lot into focus for me. It explained why my big brother had told me to stop spoiling her and that I would be the one she turned against when she got older. His telling me this caused me to push her away instead of pay close attention to her as a big sister should have. Somehow I just know if she had told me what was happening to her, I would have listened. But I also remember trying to tell my parents about things that were happening to me, and either my clues were pitiful or my parents weren't listening closely.

The memories of seeing him holding her hand near the back bedrooms came more in focus first. And, of course, her story explained why she broke down the way she did at his burial. She explained he died without ever saying he was sorry. This made sense.

At the time, I couldn't relate to the pain she felt; everyone who had molested me was still alive. I couldn't relate to the heaviness my baby sister was under and how her life was spiraling out of control with alcohol abuse. Who really knew the truth but Ted, Cindy, and our God?

This was an overwhelming revelation. My big brother was just thirty-four years old when he passed. He was a beautiful person as far as I was concerned. He had done a lot of fast living, and I still wanted to believe that God had given him an extension of life that crazy night so many years earlier, when he swore he'd died and been given a second chance to live. That whole episode came back to me vividly while I grieved his death.

Once again, where Ted was concerned, I had to force myself to stop pondering so much. The bottom line was that I would never know the whole truth. Again I was rocked by an over-the-top story concerning my big brother.

I decided that Cindy was telling the truth. I believed that despite how Ted had allegedly abused her, she still loved him. Truth was, she struggled to love him before he passed, and it was still an open matter for her after his passing. It really would do me no good to struggle to understand this side of him, because he was gone. I couldn't communicate with him directly, so it wasn't meant to be. If I had known these accusations while he lived, I would have behaved differently toward him. I would have confronted him in an effort to know the truth.

The beauty of my relationship with my big brother was that for me, he was a great big brother, and I was better having had him in my life and having shared a real sibling love with him.

There was one more thing I know because my father told me. If Daddy had learned of this molestation back in the days when he was drinking heavily, he would have killed our big brother. Again, I am thankful for the story not coming out any earlier than it did. The sad part was how the experiences impacted my baby sister's psyche. Surely Cindy had done what some refer to as "counting the costs," meaning I believe she knew at some point that it was easy for her to carry the hurt and disdain of her experience versus bringing the whole set of circumstances on the entire family.

Once they die, what do you do with the love and respect you had for someone you later learn fooled you? I decided to acknowledge it all, forgive it all, and celebrate that love was ever present.

Not Knowing Your History Makes You Vulnerable to Painful and Unnecessary Repeats

Parental responsibility includes sharing truth and passing it on to the next generation. If during the adult/parenting years, you still struggle with your own childhood issues, drama enters from left field and asserts itself …

center stage.

CHAPTER 10

Acts 3:16

And His name, through faith in His name, has made this man strong, whom you see and know. Yes, the faith which [comes] through Him has given him this perfect soundness in the presence of you all. (NKJV)

Our Strongman

Considering Daddy's extreme alcoholism, his healing was nothing short of a miracle. He was told there was no evidence of liver disease, his mind was sharp and clear, and he loved to talk about his healing. Daddy began to read his Bible constantly. The Bible is the only book I ever saw my father read.

Daddy's life reminds me of Moses' encounter with Pharaoh in Exodus 7. In Exodus 7:9, Pharaoh says to Moses, "Well we can work signs and wonders. Tell me, can you show me a miracle from your God?" The healing of Daddy's life was real, and everything about his life and walk with the Lord from the day he stopped drinking alcohol was credible.

From the time we witnessed God restoring our father, we believed, and a healing of sobriety, love, and forgiveness was present in all of us. None of us could ever deny it, because we all celebrated it.

Sure, we have had to do some damage control from time to time, because we are a family. It was not because the alcohol surfaced but because relationships had to be repaired. Trust needed restoration.

The toughest struggles were always linked to what was rehearsed in front of us and what we experienced at 316 Wood Street. For me, it was an overabundance of low self-esteem and bad habits. It's taken decades to get past the feeling that I was less than. That sense of being less than others came from inside and outside of our home. The threat was mostly external. Daddy had always taught us, "You are just as good as anybody and no better than anybody." Daddy said it often enough for it to permanently register with me. But hearing truth and believing truth are two completely different things.

We adult children easily accepted and welcomed our father's newfound strength. We communicated often about how happy we were that Dad was finally free and it looked like for good. We knew Dad had more than conquered the diseases. But we kids who grew up at 316 Wood now ranged in age from eighteen to twenty-three. We were really just beginning to show the adult manifestations of the pain we had grown up in. Funny how Dad was getting stronger and stronger, Mom could get more rest if she would just slow down, and several of us adult children were getting our butts kicked by life in general.

Daddy began to pray for and over us. I never left any visit home without both Mom and Dad standing, holding my hand, and praying for me.

Yes, Daddy's new presence of mind was undeniable. His

soul was renewed, and his spirit had to have been, too, because what guided Daddy was not from his head; it was from the inside. It was evident to our whole family.

During this time, Daddy's mother in Carbondale, Illinois, was getting very old and sickly. Daddy decided to go downstate and stay with Grandma Steele. Mom found that very difficult to handle. Now that he was sober, he left Wheaton to go back downstate. But Mom and Dad's relationship strengthened. They traveled back and forth to spend time together, and Daddy talked and really opened up to Mom.

God's timing is just awesome. So many times as a child I wanted my father to die. I hated him, I loved him, I felt sorry for him, and I experienced rage toward him. But one thing was clear; Daddy was now sober, and the God of his life was restoring his judgment as well as foresight.

One experience Dad had downstate proved to both Dad and Mom that he was listening to a spirit of righteousness, and he was sincere about seeking wisdom from the Lord.

I don't know how it happened, but one day our father decided to finally open up to his mother in Carbondale and confront the pain he had held inside since he was a child. Daddy sat Grandma down at the kitchen table and told her he needed to share something with her. He told her he had forgiven her, but it had haunted him many years. He needed to get it off his chest. He told his mother that one day when he was a little boy, one of his older female cousins came and got him by the hand. This cousin said, "J. R. you need to see this," and she led Dad into the house. There they watched his mother in bed with another man. Daddy was crushed. He loved his father and knew his dad was away, working. But daddy kept the secret.

No matter when you forgive, you remember, and sometimes

you need to confront. Daddy was now clear of mind and needed to make peace with his mother. Daddy said his mother never really fully acknowledged what he was saying to her, but later that afternoon, he knew she had heard him loud and clear.

Dad said very shortly after he had the talk with Grandma the Spirit of the Lord told him to go get Grandma's gun and remove the bullets. Dad says he did so, but he also did something else to the gun that would prevent it from firing properly.

Daddy said later that afternoon, he was sitting at the dining room table when he sensed something was wrong. Right away he heard a "click" in his ear. He turned, and there was his mother, with a gun to his head! Daddy was a man who knew guns, and he knew you don't draw a gun unless you intend to use it. You don't pull the trigger to a man's head unless you intend to kill him. Daddy was completely shaken.

What Dad knew, and what he wanted us to know, was that he had held that pain of seeing his mother in bed with another man all his life, and as life happened to him, other issues had become unbearable. Once he joined the army, he became a full alcoholic and was mentally unable to handle much pressure. How unfortunate it is that I did not see the lesson in this at the time. It took over twenty years for me to really get what happened to my father the day he witnessed this event.

You just don't know what the person next to you is experiencing or holding on the inside. The very thing we hold onto can cause our demise. One thing is certain, once that "strongman" is set free from the prison of pain, failure, heartbreak, or any other stronghold, all things in his or her life are subject to healing. It is like a balm was applied head to toe. Daddy was once again becoming a strongman with a sound mind. Another thing I love about my dad's healing is that it was done in the presence of all of his children. Whether they were near or far, all eight of my father's biological children knew that he had been healed of the alcohol and that his love for us all was great. Each one had an opportunity to reconcile, if they so desired. I took my opportunity, and I am so glad that I did. A father's love is like no other.

Do Not Let People Impose Their God on You

And don't neglect finding Him for yourself.
Know your maker.
He's present in your story.
You know your own story better than anyone.
The power that is real in life to you is real for you.

Respect your journey.

Embrace your story.

Thank God for both.

Chapter 11

Jeremiah 3:16

"And when your land is once more filled with people,"
says the LORD, "you will no longer wish for 'the good
old days' when you possessed the Ark of the LORD's
Covenant. You will not miss those days or even remember
them, and there will be no need to rebuild the Ark. (NLT)

A New Priest

When Daddy finally accepted the fact that he was an alcoholic and killing himself, he made up his mind to get help. Life had become frightening for Daddy. Each time he attempted to stop the alcohol on his own, he suffered extreme delirium tremens (DTs). The heavy alcohol use was not going to go away gently. This illness had been thirty years in the making, and his body craved strong alcohol. Although we never saw Daddy put alcohol to his lips, I knew it was past serious once I started finding empty Jim Beam bottles under his bed and bathroom sink. But once I left for the navy, the kids at home witnessed a whole new level of the illness.

Mom continued to pray and believe Daddy could be healed from the alcohol. My sisters and brothers told me of one incident when Mom was at work and Daddy was experiencing intense DTs. The kids called Mom. Leaving work and rushing home were not possible, so she told them to put their hands on Daddy and pray for him. My baby sister and brother were teenagers then, and they knew the power that mom prayed with. So they did what they had been taught. They both pressed their hands on Daddy's body and head and prayed loudly and confidently. "In the name of Jesus … by the blood of Jesus … You *are* healed!"

Soon thereafter, Daddy begged Mom to take him somewhere he could get inpatient treatment for the alcoholism. Mom was right by his side, believing and praying every step of the way. Daddy didn't even stay twenty-four hours at the first place she took him. He called Mom. "Harriett, you need to come and get me. God is nowhere in these people's program." So Mom went and got him. The scenario repeated itself one more time. Daddy stayed a few days and then had Mom pick him up. You would think Mom would have given up, but she never did. The third admittance was a success. Once Daddy saw that this program put God as the strength, healer, and higher power, he was willing to stay until he suffered through the withdrawal process. He was finally free.

Mom had always been the one in charge of sanity in our home. The baton would not easily pass to Daddy. Mom was strong, huge in personality and strength, and her and God together were a force to be reckoned with. And she had been large and in charge a long time. It would take a few years for Mom to be submissive and trust Dad with everything. In doing so, she was finally able to retire from her position at the county board and move 360 miles away to southern Illinois with Daddy. Daddy finally was going to be the head of the household, and if Mom would only allow him to be the man, she could enter into a new type of rest.

Daddy promised Mom that once she moved to join him in southern Illinois, he would go to church. Dad was to look for a church home and be ready to settle in once Mom retired and moved down there for good. But Dad did not move fast enough for Mom. Once Mom got there, she pretty much led the charge to get them both anchored in a new church home. They chose New Zion Baptist Church in Carbondale. Our grandparents, Sylvester Bradley Steele I and Elsie Steele were part of the founding members of this church. It started in their home. Daddy was well acquainted with the church and seemed to thoroughly enjoy returning to New Zion at first. But Daddy struggled with church and church folk. I always thought he was just running from his ministry. Later, I resolved to accept that Daddy was actually embracing the ministry he had ignored in his earlier years, which was to be a priest in his own home first. Family has to come before the ministry outside of the home.

Daddy was the type of man who prayed earnestly for understanding of the Word of God, which he read for hours each day. He had a keen ability to listen intently and discern truth from error. Daddy believed God was still in the healing business, that the Holy Spirit was real, and that the blood of Jesus was able to cleanse you from all unrighteousness.

Our father had learned the power of prayer and became a real prayer warrior. He prayed powerful prayers over our mother, his adult children, and all his grandchildren. He also dialogued with all of the family.

Sometimes I found myself jealous, as I would watch Dad with the grandchildren. Bizarre. When my own children were in his lap, no problem. How wonderful. I would celebrate within myself. But those grandchildren who lived close to Dad and Mom seemed to be a whole different, crazy story. This was an issue that needed deep searching and much prayer to understand. At the end of the day, the jury was in. What would come up within my heart and mind held the truth and understanding.

When I would see Dad sober and dialoguing with the grandchildren, it would take me back. I would see our home on 316 Wood Street, and my sisters and brothers—Sherrie, Brad, Robert, Cindy—and myself. I would recall the times I longed for a father who would sit down and talk to us. He didn't pray those powerful prayers over us. What we got back then were grandparents who lived close enough to see that we needed to a prayer covering. Our grandmother, Elizabeth Gibson, carried the banner of intercession for us. She prayed her daughter's family would survive, and she prayed for our individual salvation.

The only way I arrived to that sobering conclusion was to sit down and write out the generational facts (what I knew) and watch the repeats of story emerge. Even when it came to grandchildren, my parents were doing for their grandchildren what had been done for us. How could I resent that? It felt better to walk in love instead of jealousy.

There were a few other Scriptures in the book of Jeremiah that helped me understand my father's transition from pain to priest of our family. Jeremiah 17:7–8 says, "Blessed are those who trust in the Lord, and have made the Lord their hope and confidence. They are like trees planted along a riverbank, with roots that reach deep into the water." But before that, verses 5 and 6 say, "Cursed are those who put their trust in man, who depends on his strength, and who turns away from the Lord.

They are like stunted shrubs in the desert, with no hope for the future."

The beauty of my father's journey was clear. As a family, we were finally benefiting from the presence of a father who pulled his strength from his God, and he wanted us to be blessed by that confidence, and not human ability.

Consider World Hunger

Everywhere people are hungry ... for love

Chapter 12

1 Corinthians 3:16

Do you not know that you are the temple of God and that
the Spirit of God dwells in you?

Act Like You Know

"You better act like you know!" That expression means a person
needs to start operating and behaving out of the knowledge
they already have. In other words, stop acting ignorant when
you know better. My big brother would call that "playing the
nut roll."

I had to learn this the hard way. There is a difference
between acting like you know, behaving as you know, and
actually knowing. Each day I'm still learning because I want to,
which makes the journey more enjoyable than the hard way.

When you're young, married, and a parent for the first time,
you know you are winging it. But you wake up each day to face
the challenges, because you know your parents did it, so you
probably can, too. You act like you know what you're doing. It
seems to work, because after all, you are trying your best and
giving it your all. I know I did, but I was ill-prepared.

I was mostly acting out of what was rehearsed in front of

me when I was growing up. No matter what confidence you have, you are really just coming from what you thought worked and what didn't.

The energy you project brings you and someone else together. You spend time sharing experiences and stories, often discovering your commonalities. You touch on matters of the heart, taking the time to hear each other's heartbeat. You keep your listening ears engaged. You really don't want to miss a thing of significance. We often fail to realize that living means interacting with your whole world, and those interactions impact the person you become. All of that outside relating scrambles your energy, and you bring it home with you.

What am I saying here? My point is that you have to really know yourself before sharing lifelong energy with another person. I'm trying to relate the message I received inside my heart after reading the entire third chapter of 1 Corinthians. It grabbed me that I had spent years forgetting or ignoring who I really was.

I tried to pinpoint exactly when I lost touch with my inner song. I think you automatically become vulnerable when you share so much space with another human being that you lose your own rhythm. The beats get mixed. I especially believe that pressure and desire to be a great mother, partner, spouse, and careerist added to my loss of self.

I picked apart my thought process and reached the conclusion that love is best experienced when you allow yourself to be vulnerable. But vulnerability to others does not mean you should be completely defenseless. After all, you have to have an appreciation of who you are and love yourself before you can love others. You have to spend time building and strengthening yourself. It's like tithing on you. With twenty-four hours in each day, nine to ten are spent working, six to eight hours sleeping, two to four hours for someone else, cooking, cleaning, ironing, helping children with homework, and so on. The leftovers are what you get for yourself.

I am thoroughly convinced that I had lost track of myself because I put myself dead last. I am not talking about being selfish. I'm speaking of taking care of your soul, which is the essence of who you are. In these eight years, I have come to understand the value of starting the day early with a time of prayer and study. The posture of prayer helps to make the tough days more tolerable and lends itself to the greater amount of strength needed to help the people who matter most to you, your partner and family.

The worst days have been when I did not feel like the child of God I am and ignored my own worth. The foundation for living was laid long ago, and the building required upkeep. How can you give if what you have is emptiness? The spirit is housed in this body. The mind and body must be maintained.

I have been married over thirty years. I am certain that longevity happened because I rediscovered my core values. I had to reaffirm that I am not my own; I belong to the ultimate energy source, my Creator, my God. My joy came back because I reconnected to that truth. I accepted that all things were working together for my good not my demise.

I am a spiritual being who was given a natural experience of life in this body, in this one lifetime. I belong to my Creator foremost. Naysayers were being dismissed.

Anyone Trying to Pull You Down Is Beneath You

Reverse the energy.
Reach down and pull them up.

CHAPTER 13

Revelation 3:16

But since you are like lukewarm water, neither hot nor cold,
I will spit you out of my mouth! (NLT)

Another Water Baptism

So there I was—the command's Sailor of Year—sitting in a psychiatrist's office in Sigonella, Sicily. So much for a choice; either I go to the psychiatrist or be written up for assault. Long, long story … something snapped in me. While my roommate's boyfriend was fighting with her, I tried to break it up. He put his hands on me, and I snap. I went overboard.

The psychiatrist asked, "So Sylvia, how did that make you feel to hit him?" I told her I didn't know. She was good. She just restated the question, and the dam broke. She informed me that it was obvious from the grin on my face that I enjoyed hitting that guy. Hitting him represented retribution for every man who had ever hurt me! He even represented the girl who bullied me all through grade school and junior high. He represented every time I did not fight back against a physical assault. She then very methodically helped me to understand that I had to go all the way back to the hurt of the pain caused by an unpleasant, alcoholic father. More important, I needed to stop blaming myself for my initial promiscuity, because it began with molestation and incest. I had been stagnant for a very long time, unwilling and unable to put the shame behind me. For the first time, I understood that I had not been on a fence; I had been surviving my testimony. I had to make up my mind once and for all if I believed in God and trusted him to lead my life.

A fence makes an extremely uncomfortable seat. No man knows the truth of another's heart, but I believe fence-sitters are identified in the way they live, talk, and by the fruit they produce. There is an inner struggle a person goes through when they vacillate between totaling going with God or completely relying on their flesh. From experience I know that inner struggle is not easy. Seems my biggest struggles have been in times of mismatch between my heart and my head. For me, the center of any major decision always comes down to the two choices. I have to identify who or what gets edified, my flesh or my God. The line has to be drawn at some time, identifying what remains close, inside the fence, and what stays at a distance. Some things must remain out of bounds. Self-preservation demands it. So complex or extremely difficult personal decisions have too often been painful and taken way too long. I just do not believe in burning a bridge I may need to walk or run across.

I must have stayed on the fence of uncertainty ten or eleven years! Yet, in those years of living between the two baptisms, I never fully understood why I kept up those secret sin habits. I just knew that what I felt in my heart was real. It was as if I had been chasing something invisible. There had always been a tugging of sorts on my heart, and I knew that was the spirit of the Lord. Somehow this needed to be reconciled. My heart needed to mend and an explanation needed to be provided for why I suffered so many years with sexual sin. The answers would not come for nine years, while I was halfway around the world, experiencing one of the lowest points in my life.

If I had truly settled this question at any earlier time in my life, there would be no heavy load of shame, low self-esteem, or tension. But I had been sincere about my decision to make Jesus Christ my Lord. This didn't make sense to me. It was necessary for me to go through this counseling experience. There was an important element I had never considered. I had been molested at such a young age that I would never be capable of clearly distinguishing between the time of molestation and time of willing participation. The former required forgiveness of others. The later called for a forgiveness of self.

My memory is clear as far back as the age of five. I can see vividly certain times when prayer, a "protective hedge," had to have been around me. I did not start on the fence; I started inside the fence. It rains on both sides of the fence. The years of tears that followed were like a warm and heavy summer rain. It would take quite some time to dry out and heal.

This was a baptism of tears.

Sometime after this experience, I went back in my Bible study to reread the book of Revelation. The first four chapters of Revelation came alive to me in a way they had never before. The book of Revelation had always been difficult for me, because it contains much figurative and symbolic language. New for me was an understanding of the letters written to the seven churches. Suddenly, I saw an overwhelming message of love wrapped up in series of warnings, admonishments, and blessings. I could see for the first time, although it is not hidden but in fact very obvious, that the virtues and strengths of the individual churches are pointed out as well as their sins and negative aspects. The beautiful part that I could finally see was that a clear warning was being presented to the churches. Over and over again the churches are told, "He that has an ear, let him hear," which meant, "Listen up, I'm breaking this down as a warning to you. I have my eye on you, so give ear to what I am saying to you!" The best message I could hear from the pages was that despite the failures and shortcomings of the churches, there are outstretched arms of love from the Savior. That is an example to live by. You never have to condone the negative, sinful practices of a loved one, but to throw away your love for them or to abandon them because you feel justified is just not cool. I chose to love, walk in love, pray for love, and never give up on the power of love.

My understanding of Revelation has been consistent ever since. Choose what you believe, be on one side or the other, believe or don't believe, love or don't love. But most important, make a choice and stand on it.

I made a choice once and for all then. I believed in a God of the universe that was in the beginning and will be in the end. There are some things about life that I will not debate, because there is not enough time to exhaustively study the subject. This I do know: I would rather live believing in and striving to love others as Christ did than to live and die without a hope for my spirit to sail on.

Go for It ...
You Can Do It ...
Love Yourself

An inability to define, recognize, accept, and/
or love the person in the mirror is a good
indicator that you are living an untruth.
I had to change residency of my soul.
I could not live from the outer walls of my body only.
I had to live within the inner walls of my heart.

CHAPTER 14

Daniel 3:16

Shadrach, Meshach, and Abed-Nego answered and
said to the king, "O Nebuchadnezzar, we have no
need to answer you in this matter. (NKJV)

Bow to No Other

Frank and I could hardly believe it when Dad and Mom flew to
Norfolk, Virginia, in September 1989. It was the first time Dad
had come to visit me anywhere. They came for my chief petty
officer promotion ceremony, and it meant the world to me that
they and Frank would all be pinning on my anchors.

This visit exceeded all expectations on many levels. First,
Dad was visibly shaken from the plane ride. He had not flown
since he left Korea and had told himself he would never do it
again. It had been over thirty-five years, so I felt extremely
proud of him for braving the flight and happy for myself because
he came to participate in the biggest promotion of my career.
Just knowing Dad was happy to be in our home was great.

I loved talking to my father. He was sober and only getting
stronger. His stories were often comical, and his laugh took our
laughter to another level. Even the grandchildren smile when

86

they speak about Daddy's laugh. When he cracked himself up, it was totally hysterical. At the end of an outburst, Daddy would let out this sound, "keeek, keeek, keeek," which was usually followed by, "Oh me." Then he would start the hysterics all over again, and you found yourself laughing until your stomach hurt. I miss that laughter so much.

Daddy was grounded in his healing and sobriety, and he looked so good. He did not waiver, and he loved to talk about his assurance. Daddy enjoyed conversation period. I get that from him. But where his sobriety was concerned, there was an abundance of naysayers and skeptics. It really seemed Daddy enjoyed proving people wrong about him. After all, the saying goes, "Once an alcoholic, always an alcoholic." This was a concept our father totally rejected. Daddy said God healed him completely, and that didn't leave room for remnants of the disease. His mind had been healed. He was humble and often moved to tears when he spoke about his deliverance from alcohol. He would quickly remind anyone that Isaiah 53:5 says, "By his stripes we are healed." Daddy soon convinced us all that he meant business. It was a pleasure to wave the banner as evidence of God's healing power. When the Creator does it, it is well done.

There was no further need for anyone to challenge Dad on the matter of alcoholism. He was sober, he loved our mother, and he felt he was blessed by every one of his children. That sealed it for me also. God had definitely answered Mom's prayers. They had definitely been through the fire and not been consumed. Dad also understood Mark 3:27: "No man can enter into a strong man's house and spoil his goods, except he will first bind the strong man, and then he will spoil his house."

The strongman was back, but some problematic seeds had been planted, and seeds grow or die.

Daddy told us that once he was sober, his friends soon kicked him to the curb. Cold Steele had turned red hot for the Lord, and it was not debatable as far as he was concerned. Initially, Dad's old drinking buddies would stop by the house, and he would go out and sit with them for a while. But things were different, and they grew tired of Dad going on and on about how the Lord had healed him. His election was sure.

Dad had told me all this before, but during this visit, he wanted to share much more with me. He and Mom sat me down and told me how proud they were of me. There I was, thirty-nine years old, and my parents were telling me the story of how they met, how they were not married when I was born in Freeport, Illinois, and what my birth represented for them. They actually thought I didn't already know I was born out of wedlock, but I had found their marriage license one day while rifling through their dresser drawers. I told them I already knew that but thanks for sharing. Then they told me how I was the glue that kept them together initially. Daddy said he swore when I was born that no one would ever take another child of his from him. They finally married a year and half after I was born. By then, they had one more daughter born out of wedlock.

Suddenly, a couple of strong memories made perfect sense to me. For one, I remembered how my father would say things to me like, "This is all your fault," when he and Mom argued. I never understood how their issues could be my fault. But now I figured he was just expressing the fact that he felt stuck in the marriage at times, and I was the child that sort of sealed the deal in tying him to Mom. So sure, blame me.

Hearing how much attention he paid to me as a baby made me wonder if it was possible the attention he gave me as an infant was related to the craving I had for male attention. When Daddy was loving and sober, I was secure with him. That was confirmed when he told me how he would lay me on his stomach, and we would both fall fast asleep. It was funny. He said he was often drunk, so the alcohol fumes probably put me to sleep. Do you think? But security came because Daddy was so big and strong and was serious about protecting his family from outside threats.

It was a very special visit. Mom and Dad brought some healing for me. Emotionally, I had a long way to go. It made me even more curious about their life together.

The night I had to report for navy chiefs' initiation, Dad asked me what the initiation consisted of. He wanted to know what it was all about. What would we be doing that night? I told him how the chiefs would torment us all night and make us do stuff we didn't want to. Our theme was the *Wizard of Oz*, and my character was Toto, the dog. Daddy didn't think that was funny at all. He told me how he had gone through a type of initiation when he became a Mason many years before. Something he said has stuck with me ever since. He told me how he was a Mason, and Mom had been an Eastern Star for a few years, but they left it behind once they realized that anything done in secret was not of God. He said not to let anyone do anything to me that was against my faith. I liked that advice, and since that night, I adopted his attitude about secrecy in any organization.

At one point in my chief initiation, there were a couple of chiefs who insisted that I get down on both knees and bark like a dog. At first I refused. Then I got down on one knee and barked. My father's words were fresh in my mind, so I refused to get down on both knees for anybody. From that night forward, I decided I would be like Shadrach, Meshack, and Abed-Nego and bow to no man, only to my God. This commitment has served me well. I have learned that God is the only thing that is awesome, and no other force or entity could ever do what God has done for me.

There is a posture of praise and worship, and that posture is reserved for God and God alone.

If There Is a Religion, It Is the Religion of Christ

It is the religion of love.
It is an overflow out of the abundance of a committed heart.

CHAPTER 15

2 Corinthians 3:16

Nevertheless when one turns to the Lord,
the veil is taken away. (NKJV)

Beyond the Veil

Several military services have programs where troubled service members go for encouragement and personal growth. The 4-H campsite in Wakefield, Virginia, is one such site where navy personnel can go. My first experience with the program was to attend a marriage retreat in Wakefield. Soon after the marriage retreat, it was apparent that I needed additional help from a personal growth retreat.

For the personal growth retreat, I was all alone and broken. I was seeking relief and clarification. What I received April 8–11, 1999, exceeded all expectations. The heaviness on my heart was like a cast-iron lid on top of a simmering stew. The heaviness covered me from head to toe. The accumulation of years of pain was working its way to a roaring boil.

Shortly after arriving at the camp, the group was informed that the weekend experience would happen naturally if we allowed ourselves to trust the process. How healing could come at a retreat in the wilderness over the course of three and a half days was beyond me. There was nothing to lose, so I quickly tried to let go. Listening with my ears and heart allowed me to trust the process. The problem with that plan was that I equated trust with vulnerability. In my mind, vulnerability with strangers equaled a grand recipe for disaster and loss of protected airspace.

The afternoon of day 2, we were given an assignment to walk the 4-H grounds for an hour, alone, speaking to no one. The task seemed simple enough, because the grounds were big and beautiful. I could stare out at the lake for a half hour easy. The scary thing was I would be alone with my thoughts, and that meant confronting the confusion in my head. But the walk was good. It reminded me of my Girl Scout and Pioneer Girl days when I was much younger. The great outdoors was soothing. The walk into nature, alone in a safe environment, started the process that I was to trust.

As I walked around the backside of one of the cabins, I noticed a huge spider web in the corner of the under beams. It was unbelievably large and seemed to pull me in. I moved in real close. Standing directly in front of it, staring, it practically spoke to me. Until this point in my life, there had been few experiences where I heard an inner voice so prominent. The voice seemed to come from the outside of my body and flow directly into my ears. This was one of those times you don't forget.

Staring at the spider web, my first inclination was to find a big stick. I did. The intention was to use the stick to destroy the massive web. But while moving in closer, preparing to stab at the web, to rip it down, I noticed there were two flies and two smaller spiders trapped inside the web. As I paused and starred, it occurred to me that some pretty large spider had spun that web. Then, from somewhere inside of me, I heard, "This is like your home, and no one has the right to come in and destroy it." I was simply blown away. It was a relevant and timely revelation for me. It was time to really fight for my sanity and my family.

Part of the massive web that existed in my head was the sense that someone on the outside of my family was threatening to destroy the family life my husband and I had built. The threat was not to take over my family as their own but to simply destroy it, because they were close enough to do so. The destruction would have been just as I had intended to do to that spider's web—mess it all up, simply because I had gotten close enough to do so. There was a breaking inside me. I let go of tears I had never shed before. It became obvious that I never allowed myself to comprehend and process the mess that was my life. My confusion was grounded in a sense of helplessness. That moment was meant to teach me something big. The experience was an intentional part of the process I needed to trust. It was an intentional part of my destiny.

I put my big stick down and walked away toward the water.

Later that evening, we sat in a big group circle and prepared to share our individual experiences from the earlier walk. Within me I decided there was no way I would or could talk about a spider web teaching me a lesson, but I could not get it out of my mind.

The atmosphere of the group changed drastically, and people began to open up about the issues that brought them to the personal growth retreat in the first place. Many admitted their fear of facing inner demons. Issues of substance abuse, alcohol, child abuse, and leadership came up. You name it; we seemed to have it covered with that group. One man's story hit me in a way that stirred an issue that had plagued me from early childhood. I knew it was time to face these particular demons.

The counselor gave us tools to help bring about resolution. We could write letters to the people who hurt us. I knew letters would never be the right fit for what I needed to get out of me. Through tears I asked the counselor if I could do a little role-play scenario. He said yes, so I asked one of the younger ladies to join me in the middle of the circle.

I asked the girl to just sit there. She didn't have to say a word, but as I spoke to her, her name would be Jeanine for the sake of this exercise. Jeanine is my daughter's name. I needed to rehearse a talk that needed to happen with my daughter. With many tissues in hand I began to talk.

It was important to go through this process for several reasons. My healing depended on my ability to admit my issues out loud. I had to face my demons and call them what they were. I sincerely believed this type of confrontation was necessary to manifest a breakthrough from the curse of molestation and rejection, and to overcome the pain the curse had caused. I did not want what happened to me to be repeated in my daughter, who was now about eleven years old. I wanted with all my heart to create a new type of relationship with my daughter and operate from a power base of wisdom. I had to be honest, open, and vulnerable with my daughter for her to know I meant business about loving and protecting her, and breaking this stronghold. I did not want to pass to her what had been passed to me. I wanted to communicate that from my heart to my daughter's heart. This was critical to my healing process.

The role-playing helped me shape my words carefully and rid myself of excess tears.

After the session that evening, many people came up to me and said they were deeply touched by my story. Several of them, even men, told me they found the role-playing helpful and would use it in their own lives. One girl in particular enlightened me by what she shared with me. She asked if I realized that while I talked and cried, I was making flowers out of the tissue I held in my hands. She said she watched me do this the whole time I was opening up in the center of the circle. She said I continued to do so once I went back to my seat. I had no idea this was happening. She said it meant something. She said she believed that in the center of the pain in our lives, among the weeds, flowers are planted. She said our heavy tears water those flowers.

I had indeed trusted the process. More important, I had trusted God's process. There was only one way I could have lived through this heaviness. It had to be a divine hand on my life. For once, my career was not fulfilling me. School was a struggle. My Virginia Beach church was a rock of encouragement, and I loved the preached Word, and prayer groups, but I had been incomplete. I wanted to give my children more than I had already given. I wanted to give them the gift of truth to help illuminate their journey.

In order to bring and keep me together now, I had to go back and embrace the child I was then. It was important to continue to trust. If God lifted the veil, He could hold me together as I accepted what was beneath and behind that veil. This was a journey I had to go through alone before it could be shared with anyone.

Even as I write this now, I struggle to go into details. Not because I am still bound, but because I have let go of so much that I don't want to stir up old memories and revisit dark places. However, this is a story that must be told. This is a story that no longer grips me. This is a story I believe will help free others. I sought relief, but I received lasting healing from darkness that had haunted me over three decades.

So many times I have read Romans 8:28: "and we know that God causes all things to work together for good to those who love God, to those who are called according to His purpose" (NASB). This Scripture is easy to accept when you've already been through the valley and live to tell of it.

My daughter needed to know of my childhood sexual molestation. I wanted her to know that it started when I was as young as five years of age and continued until I was about twelve years old. She needed to know that it was incest and was not just one person or two, but three male family members. Most important, I needed her to understand the shame I carried went beyond victim to the reality that I had become a very willing participant. The ultimate goal was to ensure my daughter was knowledgeable of the sexual strongholds that had passed to me and be encouraged to be on guard.

This was critical, because I grew up in a whole different time than my daughter. Fear prevented me from going to my parents. Shame hindered me from admitting what I had experienced and how it affected me. There would be no reason for my daughter to fear talking to me, and I would commit to being both vulnerable and available to my children.

Retrospect

Negative pain can transform to positive learning.

CHAPTER 16

Luke 3:16

John answered and said to them all, "As for me, I baptize
you with water; but One is coming who is mightier
than I, and I am not fit to untie the thong of His sandals;
He will baptize you with the Holy Spirit and fire."

Mightier Than I

Something powerful happened Thanksgiving of 2006 that
led us sisters—Sherrie, Cindy, and myself—to get closer and
real with one another. Sherrie and I promised Cindy that we
would never again allow space to come between us. We had
no idea how much that promise would mean to the three of us.
God is faithful, and He restored the sisterly bond. From that
time forward, we grew to accept one another as adults, and
we became free enough to share as women growing in grace.
I began to really understand how Sherrie had always been like
a bridge between Cindy and me. After all, when I left home,
Sherrie and Cindy grew closer and closer and learned to lean on
each other in raising their children. Sherrie was like the luscious
creamy center of an Oreo cookie. Slapped in the center, Sherrie
was the adhesive that allowed Cindy and me to reconnect.

From then on, we came together every chance we got, and we supported each other unconditionally. There was a new maturity among the sisters. We could be honest and open as never before. As adult women, we understood the issues we had wrestled with in our formative years at 316 Wood Street and how it impacted where we were now with our own families. We were all from the same mold, and we were okay with that, because we were finally at a place where the struggle was appreciated and the election to walk in love was our collective choice. We actually engaged in fruitful conversation.

The memory of September 26, 2009, has a bittersweet sting. The celebration of Aunt Vickie and Uncle Willie's fiftieth wedding anniversary was beautiful. The Gibson family had actually witnessed another fiftieth wedding anniversary celebration. Thirty some years earlier, Grandma and Grandpa Gibson celebrated their fiftieth. The smooth and delicious taste of Grandma's homemade peach ice cream can still be summoned in my mouth (so many memories are tied to food). Grandma and Grandpa's celebration was at their home at 1518 Hill Avenue. Now, Aunt Vic was realizing the dream of unity that a fiftieth wedding anniversary brings. God had been faithful. Mom and all of my sisters and brothers were there. Because we live so far from family, these visits home are always appreciated, so we try not to miss them. Many cousins and all aunts and uncles were there. We all had a good time. Just being together at something other than a funeral was good for us collectively.

During the dinner, Cindy commented that she kept feeling shocks in her face, and there was some numbness also. By the end of the weekend, Cindy was hospitalized, and it was discovered that she had been experiencing mini-strokes. Within two weeks she was diagnosed with stage 4 non-Hodgkin's lymphoma. We were floored. Just floored. But what the God of our faith did for our family was above and beyond our collective call or cry.

There were many ups and down throughout Cindy's cancer treatments, and her frustration was evident to me from a distance. Baby sister was literally fighting for her life. Her husband was fighting for the life of their union. Our mom was fighting for her reality. In my home, we were just plain fighting.

Although I was always available via the phone for Cindy and we spoke extensively about her struggle, it was not enough. Too much seemed to be resting on the shoulders of sister Sherrie and Cindy's adult children. But to be totally honest, I knew it was finally a time for me to be a friend and not big sister. It felt as if I wasn't pulling my share of the load. In reality, I was where I was supposed to be.

In the summer of 2010, Cindy decided to submit to an experimental type of bone marrow transplant procedure. She contacted her only brothers and sisters who could possibly be both a match and in a position to handle the donor process. That was Sherrie, Robert, and me.

When the package from Barnes Jewish Hospital arrived, I was bewildered. If I were enough of a match to help Cindy, how could I possibly do so when I had so much going on in my own life? Frank had just been diagnosed with prostate cancer and would be undergoing a prostatectomy in the same time frame Cindy would be undergoing the bone marrow transplant procedure. There were several other stressful issues, but the prostate cancer was front and center.

I had a long talk with Cindy, and she understood where I

was mentally. By the time we had that discussion, Barnes had determined that Sherrie was the best match, and she agreed to go to St. Louis and endure the process for Cindy. Thank God! That was an answer to prayer.

For the first time in our relationship, I saw that Cindy was stronger than I was on many levels. Where my faith had become stagnant, Cindy's faith was advancing in leaps and bounds.

Each time Cindy came home from the hospital, we rejoiced, only to be disappointed when complications would arise, and she would have to be rushed to Heartland Hospital in Carbondale or Barnes Jewish in St. Louis.

Our mother was now eighty-one years of age, and her faith was just as strong as when we were children. But the pressure on everyone, especially Cindy and her husband, was overwhelming. Cindy would tell anyone who questioned her progress that she was not moved by what she felt or saw in the mirror. Her faith in God was solid and unmovable, and it would be best if they would believe it as well. She said, "Healed by the blood of Jesus," is what she heard within herself; it was not debatable. She believed in a mighty God who knew what she was up against.

Strength

The Father's gym is always open.

CHAPTER 17

1 Timothy 3:16

By common confession, great is the mystery of godliness:
He who was revealed in the flesh, Was vindicated
in the Spirit, Seen by angels, Proclaimed among the
nations, Believed on in the world, Taken up in glory.

Never the Same

My assignment was to keep Mom while Sherrie and Cindy underwent the bone marrow transplant procedure. Mom would stay in Huntsville about two months, or however long it took before Cindy was able to come home. Mom was most comfortable with Cindy, and in reality, Mom wanted nothing more than to return to her own house in Carbondale. We all knew that would never happen, because she was eighty-one and showing signs of the early stages of Alzheimer's or something similar. We weren't certain what was going on with her. We really needed a doctor to clarify her condition.

Mid-December 2010, Sherrie, Cindy, and Mom drove down from Carbondale and meet me halfway, just north of the Tennessee/Kentucky state line. I drove up from Huntsville, Alabama, alone. We were able to spend about forty-five minutes together, enjoying lunch and talking fast and furious as we always seemed to do. When it was time to go, I got my first glimpse of what Cindy had been telling me I needed to observe about Mom's behavior.

When it was time for hugs, kisses, and "See you laters," Mom watched me put her luggage into the rental car. She came around to the driver's side of the car, hugged me, and said, "See you later, Sissy." Shocked, I told her she was going with me. This seemed to confuse her a bit, but she quickly accepted the reality that it was actually Sherrie and Cindy she needed to say, "See you later," to.

I wish we had taken pictures that day. We sisters usually thought to take pictures whenever we were together with Mom. It was a tradition we started back in 1993. But this day we were all overwhelmed with completing this mission of handing Mom off so Sherrie and Cindy could get on to St. Louis. It never occurred to any of us to take a picture together. Besides, one sister, Pandora, was not with us. The point is, I really wish we had taken pictures that day. It was the last time I would see my baby sister walking around vibrant, laughing, and smiling. Baby sister looked good that day.

At St. Louis Barnes Jewish Hospital, Sherrie and Cindy went through intense medical procedures and continued their sisterly bonding. I can never know how hard this was on my sisters, but I do know the journey did not unfold as all of us had hoped it would.

In the beginning, Mom and I could call up to the hospital and get updates from the nurses. We would give Cindy's pass phrase, "Healed by the blood of Jesus." But soon, the hospital staff stopped giving us information over the phone, pass phrase or not. Our faith was tested but did not fail. Every day we all needed new mercy just to get through the day.

It was so unusual to have Mom in our home for more than a week. Mom ended up staying with us about two and a half months. She was a challenge. First, she was her same old self, whispering to Cindy and others on the phone about how she was ready to leave my house. I had grown accustomed to this behavior from Mom, but this time I felt as if I were holding her hostage.

Mom and I were able to get to church a few times, and we both enjoyed that. In looking back now, I can see where Mom was still looking at my family with concern, concern that we looked "better" from a distance, but up close, it was still obvious that we did not put the emphasis on God she felt should have been there. Mom and I had time of Bible study, and even that was different from any other time she and I had spent with Bibles open. This time, Mom struggled to find Scripture and seemed more interested in talking and asking questions. I enjoyed that, because Mom was the one who taught me to read my Bible and visualize with spiritual eyes. If you didn't understand something, she said to ask God to reveal the answers. Mom said when she read her Bible, it was like she was watching a movie in her mind's eye. I loved that. It worked for me.

In mid-February 2011, Sherrie came to Huntsville and stayed about a week and a half. Cindy was still in Barnes Jewish Hospital, but Sherrie's part was complete, so she was free to come get Mom. Our mom was so glad to know she was leaving. The timing of everything was bizarre. In Huntsville, our cousin's husband had passed suddenly, and Sherrie arrived just in time for his funeral. This took all kinds of wind out of us all, and we just needed each other.

About five days after the funeral, Sherrie and Mom boarded the Greyhound bus. The pictures of Mom that day are just vibrant. She was so glad to be leaving Huntsville, she could have run and shouted. I thought it was a bit comical, but I was okay with seeing her leave, because she was with Sherrie. Mom really wanted to see Cindy. She had gone from staying at Cindy and her husband's house every day to not knowing what was going on with Cindy in the hospital and not understanding why she couldn't go home to Carbondale. We all knew it was hard for her to deal with all the change. Actually, Mom had worn me out, and I needed a rest!

Within a few days, our oldest sister, Pandora, took the train down from Chicago to St. Louis, and she, Mom, and Sherrie visited Cindy in Barnes Jewish Hospital.

Pandora, Sherrie, and Mom stayed in the hospital with Cindy three or four days. I wish I could have been with them, but again, the timing was off. I was able to speak with Cindy by cell phone, but that soon stopped, and I would have to go to St. Louis.

After leaving Barnes, Sherrie, Pandora, and Mom went home. This time, Mom would be staying with Sherrie and her husband. Mom's health seemed to deteriorate rapidly. She got pneumonia and experienced a couple of falls. Then when Mom went to stay with our youngest brother at 316 Wood Street, she experienced a mild stroke. From then, everything changed for all of us.

Cindy was in Barnes Jewish Hospital, experiencing some major complications from the bone marrow transplant. Her body was at war with the new blood, and graft versus host disease was wreaking havoc on her internal organs. Her skin was turning black, and there was a lot of swelling.

The day Cindy learned Mom had suffered a mild stroke was the day we all learned the graft versus host disease had rotted away at approximately two and a half feet of Cindy's small intestine. She had to undergo emergency surgery. The intestine had separated from the base of the stomach. In addition to the partial intestine removal, bloating, and jaundice, her heart, lungs, and kidneys were all under catastrophic attack.

It was past time for me to see my baby sister, and now it was urgent. I drove from Huntsville, Alabama, to St. Louis alone. My baby brother, Robert, recognizing the urgency, got time off work and arrived in St. Louis the next evening.

We were double-armed. I carried Daddy's Bible, and Robert had Mom's. We responded as we were taught and as we knew to stand and pray. We prayed and sang and spoke to Cindy. Even if we had to shed a few tears, we kept on standing, praying, and speaking God's Word over her.

When we arrived that first day, a nurse informed us Cindy was in a medically induced coma. They explained that she was so heavily medicated, because she would not be able to endure the pain otherwise. It was so hard to watch her lying there, swollen beyond anything we had ever seen before. She was also very dark, nearly black in the face. Her arms and legs were very light in color. Jaundice was setting in. Her eyes were yellow and swollen. When she opened her eyes, she just stared at us. But we knew she could hear us.

Robert was beyond strong, as always, but I knew his heart was heavy and breaking. Robert and Cindy were the youngest, and they had a history of loving each other in a way the rest of us would never know. They were Mom's heart, separately and together. Mom was like Cindy in that she loved her babies, and both Robert and Cindy had always been precious to Mom. I was so grateful for Robert's strong prayer and comfort during this difficult time.

Robert and I stayed two more nights and then we decided to drive together to Wheaton. Robert needed to get back to work, so I decided to go to Wheaton with him. I would visit Cindy again on the return trip home. As things turned out, Sherrie drove back from Wheaton to St. Louis with me. We decided to play it by ear and remain in St. Louis until we felt an inner release to leave. It worked perfectly, as Sherrie also arranged for the two of us to stay at Hope Lodge, which is maintained by the American Cancer Society and in close proximity to Barnes Jewish Hospital.

When Sherrie and I checked into our assigned room, it had a terrible smell. There was no way we would be able to tolerate the smell, so we asked to change rooms. We tried to be strong. It was pretty obvious that Sherrie was filled with thoughts of how she and Cindy had stayed at Hope Lodge just a little over a month earlier. Cindy was full of life and hope when the two of them were last at Hope Lodge.

I had never experienced anything like Hope Lodge before, so Sherrie handled all of the logistics of our stay there. There were many friendly people who recognized Sherrie and asked about Cindy. This was an unforgettable experience, and my heart felt the pain, suffering, strength, and hope of all of the people there.

On our way to Cindy's hospital room on Wednesday, May 11, 2011, Sherrie and I stopped by the gift shop and purchased a diary. We decided to write down our thoughts to save them for Cindy to read once she recovered. That day Sherrie and I wrote:

From Barnes Jewish Hospital St. Louis MO

I wrote,

> Sherrie and I returned from Wheaton yesterday evening. We spent time with Cindy in prayer mostly. Aunt Vicky called and prayed on speaker into Cindy's ear. What a powerful warrior/ intercessory Aunt Vic is! Cindy heard her, she heard us all; we know because she reacted. Cindy pressed to open her eyes and she did so at least 3 times (from one-third to one-half open). Sherrie said she could feel Cindy wanted to leap from the bed. Cindy even moved her hand. We are standing in the gap, interceding on her behalf.

Last night we had to change our room assignment at Hope House … guess what!? Sherrie and I are "Living at 316!"—Sissy, 11:40 AM, 5/11/2011.

Sherrie wrote,

> May 11, 2011:
>
>
> Feeling truly blessed to be here @Barnes today. Thankful to spend this time with my baby sister; She knows we are here, praying for her, standing with her and being strength to her. It's nothing

like it was months ago when I was here with her. We talked, laughed, joked and enjoyed other's company. However, I am looking forward to those days again in the near future. The trials of these past weeks and months have reminded me not to take for granted the people we say we love and care about.

I am so thankful for the peace and strength of God; otherwise, I couldn't make this journey. Thank you, Father!"

Early Sunday morning, May 15, 2011, I went down to the first floor reception area of Hope Lodge, logged onto the computer, and began writing. Sherrie said it would be my first sermon since being licensed to preach. *Only Sherrie would have come up with that one,* I thought. But it was the peace of the Lord that allowed me to write, "Moan, Hope, Wait, Yet Praise." It was inspired by the forty-second psalm of David, Paul's letter to the Romans, chapter 15, verse 13, and the prophet Isaiah's words from chapter 40, verse 31.

The closing declaration read,

> Cindy … we speak into the atmosphere this day that we have a mighty *hope* in the Lord! When we do not know what to speak, we moan as the Spirit gives utterance, we moan for you and over you, we *wait* patiently, yet with great expectancy for the hand of the Lord and the manifestation of his miraculous power. We continue to *praise* as

we *moan, hope,* and *wait,* knowing all things are working to the good for us … *because we love the Lord!!*

We declare we are in right standing with God, because we believe in the Lord Jesus Christ, who came as God in the flesh, who laid down his life, and shed his blood that we might be saved and reconciled to our God, Jesus, who rose from the dead, defeating the enemy. In Him we take refuge and put our trust. Because of Him, who has given us *great hope,* we sing and shout for *joy.*

The Lord makes a covering over us and defends us. He fights our battles for us as we praise Him!!!

About noon, Sherrie and I returned to Barnes Jewish Hospital. Our niece, Cindy's daughter Monica, joined us at her hospital bedside. We had worship experience with Cindy. We sang, we praised, we prayed, and I read what I had written earlier that morning. We all clung to our faith and held back our tears as much as possible. We definitely made sure we did not lose our composure while in Cindy's room. Although Cindy's eyes were closed we believed in our hearts that she could hear us. So whenever either of us would feel the overflow of warm tears well up inside us, we would turn our back and move away from Cindy's bed. We sang songs Mom had taught us as kids, which only made us cry more. This had to be the hardest thing we had ever done together.

But no matter how hard it was for me, I knew it was substantially tougher for Sherrie, because she had given her blood for Cindy, watched her improve, and just a few weeks earlier, all signs gave hope for Cindy's continued improvement and complete healing of her natural body.

The hardest aspect of this downturn was the fact that Cindy had been healed of the cancer. It was the graft versus host disease that had become the new and dominant adversary.

In the Word of God, the book of 1 Timothy is actually a letter written by the apostle Paul to his good friend Timothy. Timothy pastored the Christian church in Ephesus. For the Ephesus church as a whole, Paul was stressing the importance of keeping their relationship with God in the forefront. As I read 1 Timothy 3:16, I was impressed that it was a part of Paul's instruction for worship and posture.

As we spent our last days and moments with Cindy, I am convinced and humbled that we were where we were supposed to be, that she heard us worshipping the Lord and standing in the gap for her. I am confident that she had seen the glory of the Lord and traded her bed clothing for angel wings.

I also know because of our God, because of Cindy's good fight, because of her posture concerning the ability of the blood of Jesus to heal, to cleanse, to comfort, and to hold, we can never be the same. Great is the mystery of godliness, and great is the ministry of godliness. There is nothing like knowing you are in the right place and position. There are times when you should be forever changed from an experience. This time was one of those times. I am forever thankful for my baby sister and what her life spoke to me during her passing and beyond.

When Life Produces Lemons, Make Lemon Pie

I have this thing about sharing drinks, so I'd much
prefer the make a pie. The point is, relationships can
produce some lemons. Add a heap of sweetness.
Be creative and share the goodness.

My mind is chock-full of memories of the goodness. Even
the tartness of life has given me pause to say, "Thank
You, Lord, for Your sweetness was in everything."

CHAPTER 18

2 Timothy 3:16

All Scripture is inspired by God, and is useful to teach us what is true and to make us realize what is wrong in our lives. It corrects us when we are wrong and teaches us to do what is right. (NLT)

Watch the Movie

When I reflect on family, thoughts of home, Mom, Dad, sisters, brothers, church, singing, friends, Thanksgiving all come to mind. The emphasis is always on home and the importance of creating an environment where children know they are loved and nurtured in truth. I believe every generation has the responsibility to pass on a stable baton composed of positive values and accurate family history.

Think about the relay race, where each team member runs feverishly with that baton secured in their grip. There's that brief period of time in which two persons—repeatedly along each lane—have their hand on their team baton. In the moment, maybe seconds (it doesn't matter how brief), there is a touch of understanding and agreement. Both runners hold on tight. Then there is a letting go and a clinching for the next journey. The passer has to release his or her grip but not until the baton is securely delivered. When the new runner takes off, it is with power and confidence. That is what happens when the carry and pass is a success.

I prefer to think of the relay race as being like the parent–child relationship. This "passing" actually starts at conception. The male passes the seed (baton) to female, and nature expects the female to hold on tight. At a designated time, the mother has carried and must release that baby. It is not until the cord is cut that new life is expected to begin its own leg, its own journey, and its own legacy. And yet, all of these persons— father, mother, child—are part of the same team. Likewise, each team member doesn't feel the full effect of the race until the last team player reaches the finish line. Each team member has his or her own race to run, but the run is only a portion of the big picture. Our lineage (the race) will keep going until the Creator ends the race. You might think the race for the individual runner is over with the end of his or her segment, but I prefer to look at it from a different perspective. My earthly biological father may have departed this life, but his love, teaching, and legacy continue to live. They live in me, and I know it.

Parents have such a short time to hold onto their children. The children are extremely blessed if both parents take the responsibility to instill in them good morals, structure, security, and discipline. There comes a time when parents must let go and pray that young adult child's journey is off to a confident start.

A healthy church environment has an important role to play in the growth of a family. Like so many, I grew up in church. We weren't allowed to run the streets at night. Nearly every evening of the week was spent in some church. We visited many different churches and associated with young people from the suburbs to the inner city of Chicago. At our family church, we spent a lot of time in the choir loft, the church basement, parking lot; it really didn't matter. The church was like an airport hub that provided so many of our needs and kept us busy in one way or another. Mostly we were always singing. Our mom (Mrs. Steele aka Tubby) was the primary church organist. We never saw anything but respect toward our mother, and she was highly regarded among the youth in our community. Mom always said, if you can talk, you can sing. So armed with that conviction, she encouraged everybody to make a joyful noise. Of course, I never realized how Mom was passing the baton even then. She was using the gifts that she was given and saving our lives and minds at the same time. Mom understood her purpose, and better yet, she was upholding her end of the covenant between God and herself.

Today, I honor my father as the most beautiful, wise, and humble man I've known. But back in the day, I feared Daddy. I saw him as a bigger than life, intimidating, dark cowboy, and he was a pistol for sure!

For many years I wrestled with Scripture. Understanding that I was chasing the God of my parents, I eventually had to accept the God that had revealed Himself to me. My parents provided the framework, and many others reinforced the structure, but ultimately it was my own understanding that had to win out.

I arrived over time, after a lot of time and after I adopted the slogan "Watch the movie." One day it occurred to me that life was so like a movie, with purpose, plot, theme, all that. But the biggest difference was you had one shot, each moment of each day. No one was going to yell, "Cut," so what you saw was what it was. If some scenes repeated themselves, you probably didn't get what you should have from it the previous time. If you missed it, well, you just had to hope you'd get a chance at it again. But one thing I was sure of was we each have our movie, and all things in our movie work together to complete who we are and what our purpose of existence is. Many things that we survive were meant to enhance us, make us better, and move our story along. Our personal movie is a lot like Scripture. There are things that instruct us, profit us, correct us, and inspire us. For sure, all things in our lives are cohesive for our survival.

I believe that whether you believe in the God of the Holy Bible or some other higher power, the greatest energy of this life comes with the acceptance of a greater force at work above, within, and beyond your physical being. I think when you tap into that energy, it improves your story and allows you to tap into an energy that has been in motion from the beginning of life as we know it.

Identify
What You Were Born to Do

Hear your inner voice.
The artist must paint, the poet must write,
the musician always has music in his being,
and God's Word
must accomplish what it was meant to do.

Listen up ...
The Father is calling your name

Read 1 Samuel 3:16

Chapter 19

Ephesians 3:16

He would grant you, according to the riches
of His glory, to be strengthened with power
through His Spirit in the inner man.

Get Understanding

So what is child sexual abuse (CSA)? My therapist said it mattered that my perpetrators were not adults, if they were older than me and abused me for their own sexual stimulation, it was abuse. This is important, because part of the healing process for a CSA victim is acknowledgment of the abuse. Some would dismiss the possibility that sexual abuse occurred, because many children naturally experiment with kissing, petting, and even sexual intercourse at very young ages. I can agree that this is often the case, and this is the position my mother took when I finally told her about my own experiences. I wrote my mother's reaction off as yet another great act of denial. In turn, I think she wrote my information off as drama or an attempt to blame her for not shielding me from the abuse.

There is a line between childhood experimentation, inquisitive behavior, and molestation. I do not believe it to be a thin line. I believe it is distinct and definitive, although I have no clear recollection of when that line was initially crossed.

There are predators, and there are perpetrators. In my case, the predators were so close, and my parents were so preoccupied, that they never even suspected a thing. The years of abuse gave way to a conditioning of my mind and behavior.

Once I had to come face-to face with the reality that I was a sexually molested child—an incest victim, I then had to deal with blaming myself. After all, how could it have gone on for years unless I had become a willing participant and predator myself at some point?

The truth is, at a certain age I looked for the attention and sexual stimulation. It was as if I had been brainwashed and lacked self-control. I began to seek the attention. Once I got it, I was disgusted with myself, angered by my sin, and fearful of the perpetrator all at the same time. With each stage of my formative years (preadolescence, puberty, teenage, young adult) I was haunted by memories of the sexual interactions from early childhood.

It is nearly unexplainable. How I could be such a promiscuous young lady and live with such overwhelming thoughts of fear, shame, and guilt.

I do not believe children are born promiscuous. I think they learn the behavior from someone. Someone senior to them heavily influences the learned behavior. This is where I discovered the line.

I needed understanding. I received it in a dream. It was bizarre at first, but the message was soon clear.

The dream centered at our home. Not 316 but my current home. It was Mom and Dad's home though. I was one of the children living in the house. Our parents would set the house alarm at night and go to bed. Over and over, I would awaken to find two or three males had entered the house without setting off any alarm! Crazy. How could they slip in undetected? Dad would kick them out and reset the alarm. One or two of them would reenter through some other door or window without tripping the alarm. This must have repeated three or four times. I recall seeing the doors and windows they came through. One entry in particular was at the side of the house, near the garage. The house we grew up in had no entry near the garage, but our parent's bedroom was next to the garage. In the dream, my parents were always sleeping. Mom didn't awaken at all, but Dad would get up, look around, and go back to bed as if the house was all secure. The intruders startled us but never harmed us. In the dream, I was in fear of what harm they could cause.

The understanding I received was that much of the incest and sexual abuse of my youth was undetected. Although Dad stood a kind of watch over us, intruders still got in. The intruders were family members, people he did not suspect.

Finally, I received some understanding of who I was back then and why it was important for me to let go of the shame forever.

My parents had done the best they could; they put certain alarms in place. For example, my father made sure the girls' bedroom was next to theirs. My father's hunting dogs were always pinned behind the house, close to the girls' bedroom window. My father and mother never allowed Daddy's drinking buddies at our house if he wasn't home. Most effective was the fact that our dad's reputation made it pretty clear that a person could get their head blown off if they crossed him.

But in my dream, the perpetrators kept coming in, despite the alarms. There was my clarification. It had to do with location.

You see, for me, the molestation did not begin in the house I grew up in. It began in a relative's home. It was a place no one would have suspected, because it was supposed to be a place of safety. It was mostly in my grandparents' basement, out of their view.

I am not a psychiatrist. Psychology is not my area of study. This is about personal experience.

For me, incest in the preadolescent and puberty years led to all kinds of issues—psychological, social, sexual—and what I desire most is for mothers to be present and to protect and dialogue with their sons and daughters about the presence of some people who would sexually harm them. If they live long enough, there comes a time in everyone's life when their sexuality naturally comes front and center. But a premature "opening up" of that box can lead to all sorts of undesirable issues.

My husband of thirty years will tell you that I was well into my thirties before I stopped crying during and after intimacy. It was just crazy. How he dealt with me in such a broken state for so long is unreal. Years after the birth of our two children, I was still uncertain of who I was as an adult sexual being. I was still unable to relax to a point of comfort and trust with my husband. Thank God there came a time when I had to understand it all and mentally get a handle on the competing forces that battled in my mind: the very real forces of love and addiction. It took counseling to help me understand that victims of long-term sexual abuse, molestation, and/or incest grow up to be some very wounded adults who are likely to carry very complicated emotional issues. There will be times when bad things happen to us, and we can only pray for strength in those times to both endure and come out on the other side better than before.

When I go back, I have to accept all that happened, because

I survived and grew from it all. It tested what was planted in me from my mother's womb. I look back with an awesome thankfulness for the rooting and grounding of love that came first, before the storms.

In the spirit, the importance of being properly rooted and grounded comes easy for me. I had to learn that understanding from my husband, the man with the green thumb.

One summer I planted beautiful purple flowers in the front yard. When Frank came home that weekend, he checked my work. It was a good thing he did. Totally bypassing the reading of planting instructions, the young flowers were planted half as deep as they should have been. My husband had to replant all of the flowers.

Frank patiently explained that the roots were too close to the surface, and the air would have destroyed their root systems. I did not know how important planting depth was, but it occurred to me that people are the same way.

We have to understand what we are working with. If you have been provided instructions, it is probably a good idea to read them over. The type of soil is important to ensure proper nourishment. Depth ensures a firm foundation, securely grounded and protected from outside elements. One last thing Frank taught me was you have to keep your eye on how the plants are coming along, because the environment, climate, and other outside influences can harm or alter your plants.

The Word of God provides so much nourishment and understanding. Even if you take in a little at a time, you will be better off with it than without it. We are essentially vessels just waiting to be filled.

Pouring Out

God can fill as many vessels as we bring to Him.
I am an open vessel.
Pour, Lord.

CHAPTER 20

John 3:16

For God so loved the world that he gave his only
begotten Son, that whosoever believeth in Him
should not perish, but have everlasting life. (KJV)

Residing in Love

I believe the ability to love unconditionally is birthed from
your innermost man or woman; your true spirit. This type of
love has to come from deep inside, because the outside layers
get beat down, mistreated, and damaged. It comes out of a
place that is pure. Even if you look pure on the outside, a deep,
cutting would reveal the tainting was preassigned from birth.
There are generational strongholds below the surface. To love
unconditionally, you have to be presented with the choice, and
how can you make a choice except to have known both? Love
is a choice.

Real love has to let go of weighty stuff. I used to think
real love should be light and easy to carry. How wrong! Real
love is birthed through struggle and can cause pressure so
intense that a new creation can occur. Real love is a force to be
reckoned with. Real love is power. Dynamic power not only

has an ability to blow up but can create a whole new thing. It does not give up easily, forever hoping for truth and clarity. It is not blind and does not create more acceptable reality. It deals with reality. And isn't that what I learned in reading and meditating on the Bible? That God is love, and that God "so loved the world," and that God not only celebrated his creation but grieved over it? And so I could make sense of John 3:16 and why I had to settle there.

Love has to move past what you know or accept, because if what you know about somebody is the essence of your love, you are operating from "conditional love," established at a given point in time. God cannot go against His own law. His very nature is to love His creation through the pain, through suffering, and even beyond violation.

I have learned that unconditional love takes you past what you know about someone and gives permission for growth and change. Unconditional love chooses to cover the person with the best you have to offer, no matter how the person acts or changes. Isn't that the purpose of Christ? That loving someone unconditionally means you have to let go of the debt of offense and release him or her, which in turn releases you. The person can never repay, so you as the debtor have to provide the means of payment.

Unconditional love is not ignorance. Unconditional love is not naivety run amuck. I believe unconditional love is birthed from an informed and conscious decision negotiated between the head and heart, which says, "I chose to love you for the future, which means nothing you can do in the present can override my love for you." It's all about a promise of constant and consistent adoration. That's how I see God's love toward us. Regardless of where we are in this natural journey He loves us. When He gave his Son, "on purpose," He gave out of the abundance of His love for us. It's in the Father's DNA to love His children. If it's in the Father, it's in the children.

I don't want to look all the way back to the cross to find unconditional love. I would much rather live forward, pursuing it. I am not interested in searching for it in people. I want to find and keep it in myself. I don't want my inner circle to be filled with people who are incapable of loving the unlovely, or loving unconditionally, or accepting the fact that we are all under construction. Seriously, I feel that way. That is because that would make things easier for me. Selfish or smart thinking? I say that's smart thinking. Seems to me it would cut down on a lot of unnecessary heartache and friction. If your long-term alignments are with likeminded people, with likeminded principles and standards, you would push each other up long before you would ever push each other out. I feel the same way about forgiveness, because we all are in need of the gift of forgiveness. There's just no sense in expecting to receive what you have no desire to carry. If you are not familiar with a love that loves unconditionally, you may be in danger of not even recognizing it when he shows up.

About twenty years ago, I had a girlfriend who was only close to me for about six months. I actually thought we would be closer much longer. The longer I hung around her, the more I knew our relationship would be short lived, because we did not share some fundamental beliefs. We kept talking about our differences. Maybe I just did not know how to relax and live, and maybe I just didn't want to be in a relationship where we rehearsed our differences.

Something she said about her husband caused a light to go off in my head. She said, "Why should I think my marriage will last a lifetime when two out of three marriages end in divorce?" Now that really is not a crazy statement on it's own. Truth is that when it comes to marriage these days, the odds are stacked against you. People don't seem to have the staying power to do the repeat work a lasting marriage seems to require. But what struck me was that she appeared to have a great marriage, so why make such a statement? A few years later, her marriage ended in divorce. I think there is much to be said about speaking life or speaking death into a situation.

I chose to believe loving relationships last because we choose to stay in them. We have to want to love people on purpose. We have to do what's best and correct for us. It doesn't matter what others would do. And who knows what he or she is capable of unless faced with the same set of circumstances? And is that even possible in lieu of the fact that no two people are alike? If the soul is the hard drive of the person, then no two persons are alike.

The greatest healing in the universe was available for me to grab hold of. That healing is wrapped in the powerful punch behind John 3:16.

By faith, you grab hold of a truth that leads to hope and transforms the broken self-image and inferior self-worth.

I chose to believe that God (the Creator, the eternal energy of all creation) cared, cares for even me, that He provided life experiences that unfolded to a peace beyond anything I could ever imagine for myself. I chose to set up a new camp at John 3:16.

Having accepted John 3:16, I also chose to take up permanent residency there. In living there, studying there, I found other Scripture to support a more excellent existence. John 13:34 gave assurance that the Father expects me to love others as He had loved me! That means unconditionally. With a love that forgives, accepts, and desires the best, it even works for the unlovely! And then John 13:35 takes it a step further and tells us that the love we have should be visible. So visible that people will take notice and point back to a loving God. An active love shines forward and backward. It surrounds. John 13:35 says others will know that we are Christ's disciples because of the love we show to one another. Wow! I was challenged to wrap both heart and mind around these Scriptures.

How could I be certain to draw up love if the well had been poisoned?

My answer came one morning as I watched a video of a man digging a well on his property. The video showed that is was very simple to dig a well and tap into water that is not only inexpensive but could be used for irrigation. It was made very clear that this type of water was not potable, which meant not fit for human consumption. That word swirled in my head: Not "potable" … hmmm.

What is fit for human consumption, capable of sustaining life, able to keep us is down deep, but you have to drill down deep to access its staying power. Christ, before he was raised with all power, went down deep. By faith, I believe He got up with all power to keep us eternally alive. That power was birthed foremost out of love.

My journey through the Scriptures, Genesis to Revelation, I learned that Adam and Eve failed well before their seed (children) were birthed. The seed of failure was passed to us all.

Knowledge is key. With knowledge anything can change, because of the light that truth shines on it. I found knowledge that a new bloodline was available. In actuality, it had been there all the time. The blood is powerful and can never be tainted or destroyed. It is a blood that was shed because of determined love. I pray to forever reside in the love proclaimed in John 3:16!

RSVP

Our debt of sin and waywardness was paid in full through
the sacrifice of the Holy Lamb of God, Jesus Christ.
There is an open invitation.
Paid with blood, and wrapped in love.
We will acknowledge and respond.
Now or later … we will acknowledge and respond.
He is Lord!

See Romans 14:11–12

My Father's Wisdom

You are just as good as any man, and no better than any man.

~ Thank you, Daddy!

This reflection has brought much
revelation.
We find ourselves in the Holy Scriptures.
Our story may line up with the woman at the well
(she remains nameless).
You may be the lame beggar,
a prince,
a widow,
a parent,
a child.

Wherever you have been,
Wherever you are,
No matter what you have done,
The Father's love is for you.
Embrace love ~
Seek wisdom.

~ Thank you, Father!

About the Author

Sylvia Steele-Dunn was raised in Wheaton, Illinois, and is the eldest of five children born to Sylvester and Harriett Gibson-Steele.

Senior Chief Sylvia Dunn retired in 2005, after serving twenty-six years of active and dedicated naval service. Her spouse of thirty years is CWO5 Franklin Dunn Jr. (US Navy, retired) of Charleston, Tennessee. They currently reside in Huntsville, Alabama. They have two adult children: a son, Jerrin, and daughter, Jeanine. They have an outstanding son-in-law, Sergeant Nathaniel Spence (US Army) and two precious granddaughters, Alyssa Marie and Alaya Lyn. Their first grandson Gabriel is due in February 2013.

Minister Sylvia serves as an associate minister and high school teen teacher under the pastoral leadership of Errol and Jennifer Davis at New Beginnings Christian Church in Huntsville, Alabama. She has a BA in religious studies from St. Leo University and EMBA from Troy University.